Leadership Ideology in Africa

Ukandi G. Damachi

The Praeger Special Studies program—utilizing the most modern and efficient book production techniques and a selective worldwide distribution network—makes available to the academic, government, and business communities significant, timely research in U.S. and international economic, social, and political development.

R

Leadership Ideology in Africa

Attitudes toward Socioeconomic Development

PRAEGER SPECIAL STUDIES IN INTERNATIONAL ECONOMICS AND DEVELOPMENT

Praeger Publishers New York Washington London

Library of Congress Cataloging in Publication Data

Damachi, Ukandi Godwin
Leadership ideology in Africa.

(Praeger special studies in international economics and development)
Bibliography: p.
1. Africa—Social policy. 2. Africa—Economic policy. I. Title.
HN777.D35 309.1'6 75-19772
ISBN 0-275-56760-5

PRAEGER PUBLISHERS
111 Fourth Avenue, New York, N.Y. 10003, U.S.A.

Published in the United States of America in 1976
by Praeger Publishers, Inc.

Printed in the United States of America

For my grandmother,
Udim Ukongbim Kalibe Ogar,
who first exposed me to the art
of leadership at the village level

ACKNOWLEDGMENTS

I am grateful to the many people who helped make the completion of this book possible. I want to acknowledge the contribution by Joseph Rodgers for translating most of the French documents into English. My appreciation also goes to Ode Okore and Emmanuel Osei for their research and assistance. I should emphasize that Ode Okore, using his editorial experience, also contributed by providing ideas on the structure and format of the book.

Special thanks go to Oldrich Cerny and Jean Favre who helped with the administrative arrangements during the course of this study. Equal thanks go to Benjamin Bentum and M. G. Samaki who were kind enough to share their practical experiences of African politics and development with me.

Finally, the secretarial assistance of Lucille Stephenson, Janette Ho, Diana Shorey, Sylvia Camocho, Ngozi Ibekwe, and Eva Adom is very much appreciated. Also thanks to Maryse Gaudier and Cherry Gordon for tracking down most of the documents for me.

CONTENTS

LIST OF TABLES

Leadership Ideology in Africa

CHAPTER

1

INTRODUCTION

This is a study of the socioeconomic attitudes of African leaders to development. For African nationalist leaders, political independence was merely a beginning; they became fully responsible for their new nation-states, for the operation of economies short of both capital and human resources, for the welfare and well-being of societies characterized by poverty, ignorance, and disease, and for the direction of political entities lacking cohesion. These leaders have employed various strategies and techniques to meet these problems of development, but the results have not been remarkably successful because these techniques are replete with dilemmas. Some of these techniques and strategies are the choice between industrial development and agricultural transformation; capital-intensive and labor-intensive technology; export of raw materials and domestic processing. These dilemmas implicit in the choice of techniques have led many African leaders to conclude that the necessary prerequisite to solving their problems is the provision of an ideology of development.

What do we mean by "development ideology?" Webster's Dictionary defines ideology as a "systematic scheme or coordinated body of ideas or concepts, especially about human life or culture." Accordingly, by development ideology we mean a systematic body of ideas, beliefs, and policies about the ways and means of bringing about the welfare and the well-being of societies. The ways and means may involve such things as human resource development* and the modification and eradication of old or building of new institutions. But whether the ideas are true

*Human resources, according to Frederick Harbison, are the energies, skills, talent, and knowledge of people that are, or that potentially can or should be, applied to the production of goods or the rendering of useful services. For details, see Frederick H. Harbison, Human Resources as the Wealth of Nations (New York: Oxford University Press, 1973).

or false, idealistic or pragmatic is not important in this context. What matters is that these ideas exist and are given existence by men who are usually leaders, and we call this systematic set of ideas given expression by leaders, "leadership ideology."

Many African leaders have propounded different ideologies about development; however, East and Central African leaders provide more ample material than West African leaders, perhaps because the political leaders in this region have enjoyed more stability, and more permanence, than their West African counterparts. This fact is reflected in this book, for there were more responses from among the East African leaders to the questionnaire we sent out. For example, Julius Nyerere has made a contribution, as will be seen in Chapter 5, to African political thought that has probably been influential elsewhere in Africa, as well as in Tanzania. His Arusha Declaration, "education for self-reliance" and "socialism and rural development" provide a coherent and comprehensive statement of attitudes and intentions: the priority is to be rural development; the guiding principle is to be a socialism rooted in African communal traditions; the means will be found not only in careful restructuring of the political and administrative agencies but also in the efforts of the people themselves. Kenneth Kaunda of Zambia expresses similar ideas and proposes similar actions, with a more overtly humanist emphasis. The Kenyan path to African socialism is more cautiously pragmatic and has come under criticism from radical elements in Kenya.[1] Also, for instance, the differences between Seretse Khama's "Kagisano" and Obote's Charter portray the hiatus between the conventional and the radical approaches to African development.* A common concern in all their ideologies is with the structure and operation of institutions, especially governmental bureaucracies and socioeconomic institutions.

The ideologies of West African leaders also show their preoccupation with the same problems and a similar concern with socialist solutions. For example, Nkrumah emphasizes the need for an ideology as an instrument in the struggle against hostile social and economic forces and the need to adapt political forms to meet the realities of that struggle.[2] Léopold Senghor stresses the importance of culture in the task of nation-building. Contrary to the notion of most African

---

*Obote's "Common Man Charter" was adopted by the Annual Delegates' Conference on the Uganda People's Congress (UPC) on October 24, 1969. It set out the basic principles of a socialist policy that the government intended to adopt. Shortly after the UPC had adopted this charter, it decided that Uganda should become a one-party state, with the UPC as the only party. The leader of the UPC, Milton Obote, probably drafted the charter. Obote was overthrown by a military coup, led by General Idi Amin, in November 1971: political parties were subsequently banned.

leaders, he observes that culture is not an appendage that can be lopped off without damage. It is not even a simple political means, for it "is inside and outside, above and beneath all human activities; it is the spirit that animates them, that gives a civilization its unique style."[3]

But promise is not performance; and philosophies are easier to enunciate than to put into practice. Moreover, a proclamation of good principles is not a pledge of good intentions. As a result, then, the central theme of this book is a discussion of the issues between development ideas and development actions. In short, the book seeks to provide answers to the following questions: Is there any connection between the ideas expressed by African political leaders and their political actions? Do African political leaders believe what they say?

In order to answer these questions we wrote letters to 22 African heads of state asking them to summarize for us their development ideologies or philosophies, their ways and means of implementation, and their overall goals and direction. The responses were alarmingly unfavorable, an indication that most of the African leaders themselves have not been thinking along these lines. The following leaders responded: Julius Nyerere of Tanzania sent us his idealogy of "socialism and rural development"; Kenneth Kaunda of Zambia, "humanism"; Seretse Khama of Botswana, "Kagisano"; Mo'ammar Al-Gadhafi* of Libya, "Arab-Islamic socialism"; Marien N'Gouabi of the People's Republic of the Congo, "scientific socialism"; and Houphouët-Boigny of the Ivory Coast, "free-market economy." President William Tolbert, Jr. of Liberia replied promising to send his ideology but he never did, maybe because of the pressures of his office.

Geographically, the responses are quite representative of the whole continent. North Africa is represented by Libya, West Africa by the Ivory Coast, East Africa by Tanzania, Central Africa by Zambia, and Southern Africa by Botswana. The only limitation in the geographical representation is the absence of an English-speaking West African country. It is very difficult to speculate why there was no response from any of these countries except Liberia, which made an unfulfilled promise. Maybe the leaders in these countries were too preoccupied with the heavy responsibilities of governing.

However, these responses were supplemented with personal interviews with some of the leaders who replied to our questionnaire. Also we relied on secondary material, such as government statistical abstracts, national development plans, archival sources, and relevant literature for data.

---

* This name is more commonly spelled Qaddafi in English-speaking countries.

Each of these chapters is organized under the following subheadings: a short historical review of events (where applicable) that might have influenced the leaders in formulating their respective ideologies; the leadership ideology per se; objectives based on the ideology in question; programs of action aimed at attaining the objectives so set; and evaluation of the performance or degree of development. To measure the extent of development in these countries, we use the following indicators: population and the composition of the labor force; manpower development and utilization (that is, educational development and the employment scene in each of the countries); and the social development. In this context social development is equated with the distribution of the proceeds of development or what is popularly known in the development literature as the "national pie;" the provision of housing and health facilities; the rate of literacy; and the availability and consumption of durable goods like cars, telephones, and commercial vehicles. Although we limit ourselves to these indicators, we do recognize that there are, indeed, a great many ways of measuring development and modernization.[4] We rely on the above indexes because they best meet our purpose in analyzing and evaluating the extent to which leadership ideologies have been and are being implemented in Africa.

We should point out that the book has certain limitations. Most of the statistics used in evaluating the degree of development are not up to date. Of course, it is common knowledge that in developing countries statistics are not easily available; and the developing countries of Africa are no exception in this regard.

Another shortcoming is the little or almost zero attention given to political development in spite of the fact that its major theme is "ideology." This oversight is intentional, for our main focus is the usage and application of ideology from the socioeconomic perspective. We recognize that the concept of ideology was developed in philosophical and political analysis and is now closely associated with revolutionary thought and action; but is has also become a fashionable concept among development planners and it is in this context that it is used here.

Despite these limitations, we believe the book has certain relevance. Ideologies interlock and must be carefully unwound for analysis. Accordingly, one of the purposes of this book is to unveil the gyrus of the development ideologies of some African leaders, thereby making it feasible to carry out a critical analysis and evaluation of their application and effectiveness.

Also, since the independence of many African countries there has been a proliferation of development theories and strategies. In spite of the fact that the African governments have really adopted and applied these theories, they are still underdeveloped. This gives rise to some searching questions: Are the statistics believable? Do they tell the whole story? Is there something in the sociopolitical make-up of these countries that raises more and more intractable obstacles as they attempt to advance economically? In short, is there something grossly wrong with current economic theory of development?

We believe that the socioeconomic underdevelopment of the developing countries is due largely to a lack of any ideological foundation for development. In order to have a radical change of practice, there must be a radical change of thought. It could be argued that the lack of rapid development in Africa is because most African leaders are still blindly glued to the colonial structure. Consequently, development programs are still based on this structure that in essence was meant to preserve the interests of and bolster the colonial power. For development programs to be made more meaningful in the African context, there needs to be an ideology that provides the necessary base and direction. It is hoped that this study will motivate African leaders who hitherto have been operating without a development ideology to start thinking of formulating one.

Even for those leaders with development ideologies, there has been no evaluative study of the extent to which such ideologies are implemented. As a result, we do not know how sincere the African leaders are when they enunciate various ideologies of development. One of the main purposes of this book is to provide such an evaluation, which aims at determining the relationship between development ideas and development action.

NOTES

1. Kenya, African Socialism and Its Application to Planning in Kenya (Nairobi: Government Printer, 1965).

2. For details see Kwame Nkrumah, Towards Colonial Freedom: Africa in the War Against World Imperialism (London: Heinemann, 1962), and I Speak of Freedom (London: Heinemann, 1961).

3. Léopold Sédar Senghor, On African Socialism (New York: Frederick A. Praeger, 1964), pp. xiv-xv.

4. For details on measurement, see Frederick H. Harbison, Joan Maruhnic et al., Quantitative Analyses of Modernization and Development (Princeton, N.J.: Princeton University Press, 1970).

CHAPTER

2

KENNETH KAUNDA: HUMANISM IN ZAMBIA

Kenneth D. Kaunda was born April 28, 1924 in Lubwa. In 1941 he went to Munali Secondary School, Lusaka, after which he returned to Lubwa in 1943 as a teacher. Throughout his teaching career he played a leading role in promoting welfare association in the Northern Province and in the Copperbelt.

As a result of his political activities he was elected the national secretary of the Africa National Congress (ANC). In 1955 he was imprisoned for two months for encouraging boycotting of shops and other public places. In 1958 he led a splinter group of ANC to form the Zambia Africa National Congress (ZANC) and was later elected president. The new party was soon banned and most of its leaders, including Kaunda, were imprisoned.

Mainza Chona, who later became vice president and prime minister, formed a party called United National Independence Party (UNIP), and when Kauda was released from prison in 1960, he was elected president of UNIP. In 1962 UNIP, in coalition with Harry Nkumbula's ANC, formed the first African administration with Kaunda as minister of local government. With a new constitution providing self-government he won a landslide election victory and became the youngest prime minister in the commonwealth on January 22, 1964. On August 25, 1964, he was named president designate and assumed the full title on October 24, 1964.

As stated in Chapter 1, we shall first present President Kaunda's stated ideology of humanism as well as his program for implementation and then proceed to evaluate the performance of this ideology. The performance will be evaluated under the following variables: labor force, income distribution, the state of the economy, and social development (that is, housing, health, and education).

HUMANISM AS AN IDEOLOGY

Humanism is supposed to be derived from the traditional African culture. According to President Kaunda, the African society was progressive and human, and the present generation of Zambians must bear this in mind in all its political, economic, social and cultural activities. The question to ask is, In what respect and how much will it be necessary to change the traditional African society and reconstruct it as it emerges from a nonmoney to a money status? Due consideration has to be given to the impact that the use of money has made on the Zambian society. Economists postulate that the use of money presupposes exchange and exchange in turn presupposes specialization and these three are inseparably linked in a self-generating process. It is well-known that as the money expands, such as it is fast doing in Zambia, the government is forced to push people to become more and more specialized in various fields; and as the people become more and more specialized, they become more and more effective in their fields and, all other factors being equal, the money economy will expand.

Whatever changes take place in the society, whatever sacrifices are made or urged on individuals to make, by the party and government, in the task of fighting to preserve the man-centered society, the government must remember that it is people above ideology; man above institutions. The party—that is UNIP—and government must continuously refuse to slavishly tie men to anything. Society is there because of man. In order to improve the society for man, he declares that he and his party are open to advice from anyone from any part of the world provided it is in line with their stated principles. In short, whatever the party and government undertake to do they have to remember that it is man who is the center of all human activity.

> This high valuation of MAN and respect for human dignity which is a legacy of our tradition should not be lost in the new Africa. However "modern" and "advanced" in a western sense this young nation of Zambia may become, we are fiercely determined that this humanism will not be obscured. African society has always been man-centered. Indeed this is as it should be otherwise why is a house built? Not to give Man shelter and security? Why make a chair at all? Why build a factory? Why do you want a state ranch? For what else would there be need to grow food? Why is the fishing industry there? We can go on asking these questions. The simple and yet difficult answer is MAN. Difficult, too, because Man has not yet understood

> his own importance. And yet we can say with justification and without any sense of false pride that the African way of life with its many problems has less setbacks towards the achievement of an ideal society. We in Zambia intend to do everything in our power to keep our society man-centered. For it is in this that what might be described as African civilization is embodied and indeed if modern Africa has anything to contribute to this troubled world, it is in this direction that it should.[1]

From this definition, humanism is egalitarian. It stipulates that certain things in life should not be rationed by money or power. Also it believes that things like education or health should not go to the highest bidder, but that all people have a moral right to equal opportunities.

Kaunda recognizes that although leaders preached the importance of man before independence and have continued to do so after it, this and its true meaning has not begun to permeate the rank and file of the UNIP, the civil service, the police, the army, and the general public to any appreciable extent. The key question is how can the party and government begin to inject this into the bloodstream of the nation? Besides, how can this be done without overstressing the importance of preserving the past society at the expense of the material development of Zambians? How do they preserve what is good in their traditions and at the same time allow themselves to benefit from the science and technology of their friends from both the West and East? Here Kaunda refuses to be dogmatic about anything. He asserts that his party and government are not given to the art of drawing fixed lines somewhere between any two end choices. Instead his choice is constantly to look for and devise new ways by which to encourage the hastening of material advance while ensuring that the principles of traditional man-centered society are preserved.

In order to do this, the objectives of the party are defined thus:

(a) To achieve African democratic socialism for Zambia, raise the standard of living of the people and generally strive to make the people of Zambia contented and happy. (This is being realized beyond all doubt.)

(b) To ensure acceptance of the principles of equal opportunity for all peoples in all aspects of life including wages of workers, social health and educational facilities. (We shall continue to tackle this programme vigorously.)

(c) To co-operate with any movement or organization for the improvement of workers' conditions and then secure the most equitable production and distribution of the wealth of the country in the best interests of the people. (We have done a lot, but much more remains to be done.)

(d) To co-operate locally and internationally with all African nationalist movements and parties which work for complete eradication of all forms of colonialism, imperialism, racialism, and discriminatory laws and to fight for African Unity. (This is our cardinal programme. We shall not rest until it is accomplished.)
(e) To abolish all forms of discrimination and segregation based on color, tribe, clan and creed and to maintain, protect, and promote understanding and unity among people of Zambia by removing individualism, tribalism and provincialism. (These rank among deadly vices!)
(f) To promote and support worthy African customs and cultures. (On this, the rest of the world has a lot to learn from us.)
(g) To protect and promote trade, industry and agriculture in the interests of the people by legislation and to protect the interests of commercial traders and help them in their progressive business and schemes. (We are vigorous on this programme because it gives economic opportunities.)
(h) To run and establish newsletters, newspapers or magazines in order to advance the aims and objects of the party. (We have comprehensive plans afoot.)
(i) To organize and maintain in the country and in Parliament increased membership and support for the United National Independence Party. (We are doing this with renewed vigor.)
(j) To give effect to the principles approved from time to time by the Party Conference, the National Council or by the Central Committee.
(k) To ensure that freedom of speech, worship and freedom of the press shall not be infringed and that the people of Zambia shall be free to think, speak, write, assemble, work and trade in accordance with the laws of the country. (We are working to achieve this.)
(l) To carry on any other activities which to the Central Committee may seem conducive to the aims and objects of the Party and to do such other things as are incidental to the attainment of the above objects.[2]

All of these objectives are geared toward promoting the ideology of humanism, which, if properly implemented, hopefully will lead to a developed socialist state of Zambia. The next question that comes to mind is, What apparatus or programs have been developed to attain humanism?

PROGRAM FOR IMPLEMENTING HUMANISM

In expounding his ideology of humanism President Kaunda asks these basic questions:

(a) who shall own the means of producing wealth?
(b) what shall be the means?
(c) what wealth shall be produced first?
(d) once acquired, how and who distributes this wealth?[3]

The answers to these questions form the program of action.

He realizes that to produce anything all that is needed is land, capital, and labor. It is not surprising, therefore, that in Zambia land is regarded as the property of the state. The reason for this state ownership is to prevent absentee landlordism, but more importantly

> it is to say that once people realized that no one would tamper with their land for years and years to come they would feel that certain. In other words, the incentive to develop to the full would not be there. One feels strongly, however, that land cannot be made and does not grow. From this one hopes the sacredness our ancestors attached to it (that is land)—so much so that they could not think of selling or buying it—will be understood and appreciated.[4]

Consequently, in the future no person will be allowed to own land in perpetuity or to possess an exclusive interest in the land in perpetuity. The state may rent land to various users on behalf of the people.

Industrial and agricultural development form a vital part of the program of action. The objective is to make the agricultural sector as productive and as profitable as the industrial sector, especially the mining industry. The party intends to carry out an agrarian revolution by making every village and villager in Zambia productive on the land, as well as in secondary industries based on agriculture. To do this the party will place greatest emphasis on cooperative effort, especially in respect to agricultural development, although members of cooperative societies formed to promote industrial projects would be increased progressively. Also, the party's policy of encouraging private enterprise, within the framework of accepted government policy, will continue. The government has outlined clearly the areas of economic activity over which it has complete prerogative and others that could be jointly owned by the state and private individuals.[5] Targets for industrial and agricultural production will be devised from time to time in order to provide the much-needed national incentive and to encourage realistic planning. Finally, the party accepts that a rapid and widespread improvement of living standards of Zambians depends upon hard work and maximum utilization of land for agricultural purposes.

Also, success in establishing a true humanist state will depend on cooperation and development between the party leaders and leaders of persons in all walks of life in Zambia. To achieve this the

President's Citizens College has been established to help in disseminating and promoting the principles of Zambian humanism. Moreover, Village Productivity Councils have been formed. In schools, students are to be taught the importance of collective effort in the context of the principles of Zambian humanism. When possible, school authorities must encourage school children to maintain school gardens.

The party itself has a vital role to play in order to foster humanism in Zambia. It must strive relentlessly to establish a socialist state based on the objectives previously outlined. It is therefore mandatory for all party leaders, that is, all members of the Central Committee, ministers, members of the Parliament, and all officials to declare openly their support for the principles of Zambian humanism. These leaders ought to abandon any practices or privileges that conform to capitalistic principles and adhere to the principles of Zambian humanism.

To make sure that the leaders play their role properly, President Kaunda has developed a leadership code for them:

> I do not want to see a weakening of family ties and a repudiation of our poor relatives;
> I do not want to see snobbery and intellectual arrogance;
> I do not want to see decisions made for self-interest rather than the benefit of the people;
> I do not expect to see people using wealth or superior education to manipulate decisions in their favor;
> I expect people to work hard and live a simple life;
> I expect people to save or re-invest;
> I expect people to share with their poor relatives;
> I expect people to accept the obligation to share their enterprise with the state, if it so wishes;
> I expect people with share holdings or business interests which may compromise the carrying on of their duty, to dispose of them;
> I expect people to accept adverse decisions, to wait their turn in the queue, to admit that there are more deserving cases.[6]

This code is really an extension of the principles of humanism. It emphasizes the need for hard work, self-reliance, and social justice.

EVALUATION: PERFORMANCE OF THE DEVELOPMENT IDEOLOGY

In order to make these programs work, President Kaunda recognizes the need for an administrative machinery that not only brings government to the people even in villages, but that is also manned by men and women who understand the shortcomings of Zambian social, economic, and political systems and who appreciate the Zambian values and needs. He also recognizes the fact that the system of administration that Zambia inherited from the British colonial government was more geared to support a foreign capitalist society. To redress this system, the administrative machinery has been decentralized, thereby increasing the opportunity at provincial and district levels to make decisions more relevant to the needs of the people. The impact of decentralization becomes more visible when we evaluate the Zambian development path since independence.

Population

Zambia, then known as Northern Rhodesia and part of the federation of Rhodesia and Nyasaland, gained internal self-rule in January 1964 and in October of the same year formally became independent. At independence Zambia's population was 3.6 million. By 1972, the population had increased to 4.5 million. Out of this, the African population was estimated to be 4.4 million and the non-African population 0.1 million. This shows a 2.7 percent average annual growth, which is by all standards high.[7] A pertinent question to ask here is what is the impact of this high population growth on employment. Before answering this question, it may be helpful to note the breakdown of the population between rural and urban.

The percentage of the Zambian population that was urban in 1965, a year after independence, was 20.1 percent. By 1970 it had increased to 25.3 percent. On the other hand, the rural population was 79 percent in 1965 and by 1970 it had decreased to 74.7 percent.[8] There was therefore a pull from the rural area to the urban which was possibly generated by the desire of the rural people to move closer to the pool of modernization so as to have a "piece of the action." Since the statistics show that the bulk of the population is rural, there is little wonder that President Kaunda has embarked on decentralizing the administrative machinery from Lusaka (the capital) to the villages in order to bring the government to the people. To demonstrate his concern for the rural population, he said in "The Kabwe Declaration"[9] that

> We have the major task of decentralizing the economy in favor of the rural areas. The plight of the overwhelming majority of people in Zambia's rural areas calls for an urgent and positive programme of action. We have an obligation to fight for their cause because it is our cause. . . . We must fight the war against hunger, poverty, ignorance and disease which plague the majority of families. . . .[10]

To what extent has this promise that is based on the ideology of humanism been fulfilled? It should be noted here that the percentage of the economically active population employed in the agricultural sector is 15.3 percent, which is quite low when compared with 22.5 percent for Kenya and 90.8 percent for Tanzania.[11] What has accounted for this low percentage for Zambia? An examination of the human resource "problem profile" of Zambia may provide the reasons.[12] The resource profile comprises mainly manpower, education, and employment questions.

At independence Zambia had little or no native skilled manpower. As a result, although the labor force consisted mainly of Zambians, most jobs that required postprimary education or special training were occupied by non-Zambians, especially British or South African citizens. As noted above, very few Zambians had the opportunity to go as far as secondary and even fewer had experience in responsible administrative posts.[13] Was it because the British wanted to stay and rule the country, as they have in Rhodesia, that they resorted to a deliberate policy of keeping the Zambians illiterate by creating impossible conditions? Or was it a case of the Africans not being ambitious enough to push themselves? It is not exactly clear what actually happened in Zambia. However, the following figures speak for themselves both in terms of the appalling conditions that prevailed in 1964 and the accomplishment of independent Zambia since that time.

Education

With regard to education, the number of university graduates in 1964 was 109, while that of secondary graduates was 1,200.[14] However, in 1966, in keeping with the ideology of humanism which is man-centered, it was estimated that Zambia spent about 23 percent of her total revenue on education. The result was a sharp increase in student enrolment at all school levels. Thus between 1964 and 1968, primary school enrolment stood at 608,893; secondary school enrolment increased from 9,000 to 40,000 and by 1970 the total number of secondary school graduates rose to 6,000.[15] Also by the same year the student enrolment at the newly established University of Zambia stood at 1,200.[16] It is striking that most of the primary and secondary schools built after independence are in the rural areas. The rural people are thereby accorded an opportunity of educating their children—an opportunity that was exclusively reserved for urban dwellers before independence.

Labor Force and Employment

The shortage of skilled native manpower initially had an adverse effect on employment opportunities for the Zambian labor force. For example, in the copper mines, the life-blood of Zambia, only 704 Zambians occupied jobs predominantly held by expatriates, although by 1970 the number had risen to the phenomenal figure of 4,661, thanks to Zambianization.[17]

This big increase of Zambians in highly skilled employment was achieved in spite of the fact that immediately after independence the small number of educated Zambians was stretched to fill such economically unproductive posts that could not be entrusted to expatriates as ambassadors, cabinet ministers, immigration officials, etc. The immediate result was a temporary shortage of educated Zambians to run the industrial, commercial, and mining sectors or the educational system above primary level. But the government's pragmatic policy of asking the expatriates to provide on-the-job training for Zambians coupled with a scrupulous policy of recruiting foreign experts on short contracts helped to alleviate the situation.

Such an achievement is even more impressive if we take cognizance of the fact that in 1964 Zambia already had a large modern sector that was almost wholly in the control of expatriates. The preponderance of expatriates controlling this sector could be attributed to two main reasons. The most obvious was the acute shortage of indigenous skilled manpower, especially at the inception of independence. But the strongest is that copper mining is the life-blood of Zambian economy; in 1964 it provided over 90 percent of government revenue.[18] The hidden fact was that in 1964 this industry was owned by two foreign conglomerates: the Anglo-American (which, despite its name, was South African owned) and the Rhodesian (later Roan) Selection Trust (which was American). These two were in turn linked with other multinational mining companies, finance houses, and the like.[19] An economy of this sort that depended entirely on an expatriate labor force was definitely not in the interest of the average Zambian. And President Kaunda, propelled by his ideology of humanism, has been able to correct this anomaly by providing the Zambians, through his development programs, with opportunities to share in the fruits of Zambian development.

The Zambian has therefore become the beneficiary of Zambia's development. We have indicated that in 1964 only 704 Zambians held jobs that were predominantly occupied by expatriates in the mines and that by 1970 this figure had jumped to 4,661. During the same period the number of expatriates had declined from 7,621 in December 1964 to 3,774 in 1970. Also the number of Zambians in all categories of central government employment increased from 70.8 percent in 1966 to 83.1 percent in 1971.[20] On the whole, wage employment between

1954 and 1964 was almost stagnant at 267,000. In 1970 this figure had risen to 390,000 which is rather remarkable.[21]

Economic Development

The per capita income of the Zambian has also increased since the institution of humanism as an ideology of development in 1967. In 1969 the GNP was $1,460 million. The GDP at 1954 prices rose during the ten-year period before independence by 66 percent at an annual rate of 5.2 percent or at some 2 percent per capita after allowing for population increase during the period. After independence, over the period of 6 years (1965-70) the real GDP increased by 83 percent at the annual rate of 10.6 percent or 8.2 percent per capita annually. This brought the per capita GDP to K 303* in 1970 compared with K 126 in 1964, expressed in 1969 prices.[22]

It is already clear that in spite of the human resources problems, Zambia's 1963 per capita income of $138, although a little below the figure of $140 for Africa as a whole at that time, was nonetheless the highest per capita income among all East African countries.[23] Of course, having the highest per capita income does not necessarily indicate equitable distribution.

With regard to income distribution among the Zambians, inequalities still exist despite government attempts of ensuring even distribution. There are still especially gross inequalities between the rural and urban sectors of the economy and between the African and expatriate employees. The per capita income of the 30 percent employed in the formal or urban sector is K 690 while that of the 70 percent employed in the rural or informal sector is K 70.[24]

On the African-expatriate wage differentials, the African annual wage still ranges from about one-thirteenth of that of expatriates (for example, in agricultural industries) to about one-fourth (in transport, communications, and commerce). These gross disparities in wages are owing to the fact that because of her manpower shortage, Zambia has had to attract expatriates through the inducement of high salaries.

In spite of these inequalities, wages have risen very fast since independence. In 1964 the average wage of an expatriate was about nine times that of the African; in 1970 it had come down to about six times.[25] On the average, during the period 1964-70, the wages of African employees had increased by 130 percent[26] thanks to humanism.

---

*1 Kwacha equals $1.56.

Social Development

The implementation of the ideology of humanism has also brought about social development in Zambia. Social development means improvement of social services, for example, education, health, housing, social welfare, and community development. We have already pointed out the inequality that existed, before and immediately after independence, in the distribution of income. Similar inequality existed in the provision of social amenities for both Africans and expatriates. In fact, there was a whole infrastructure catering to the needs of expatriates, especially in housing and urban services. After independence the Africans who assumed the jobs of these expatriates, or moved to comparable levels, naturally inherited this infrastructure, thereby creating a new inequality among the elite Africans and the rest.

Although black and whites are now allowed through the same doors in butchers' shops, it is not yet known what efforts the government has made to break down entirely this dual system of social amenities between "high" and "low." This dualism is definitely at variance with the principles of humanism.

The situation of public health still needs to be greatly improved, especially given the fact that Zambia's ideology of development is man-centered. In 1968 there were 5 general hospitals, 15 district hospitals, 23 rural hospitals, about 200 rural hygiene and disease prevention centers, and numerous private clinics. There were 317 doctors, that is, 1 doctor for 14,000 inhabitants.[27] These figures can be compared with those for Tanzania: 116 hospitals, 1,346 dispensaries, and 1 doctor for 20,000 inhabitants; and Kenya: 199 hospitals, 162 health centers, 500 dispensaries, 1,076 doctors, that is, 1 doctor for 9,500 inhabitants. The figures are not that impressive. The picture may have changed since then, but there are no statistics to prove it.

But the Zambians seem to be doing better with regard to ownership of durable goods. For example, there are 49,700 cars, 20,000 commercial vehicles, 43,267 telephones, 80,000 radio sets, 15,500 television sets, and 577 kilograms of consumption of power per head. These figures are more impressive when compared with those of Nigeria with a population of about 15 times that of Zambia: 73,000 cars, 31,000 commercial vehicles, 77,880 telephones, 12,250,000 radio sets, 52,500 television sets, and 32 kilograms of consumption of power per head.[28] One point can be deduced from these figures on health and durable goods: the government seems to put more emphasis on durable goods or what we may call externals of modernization than health.*

*Externals of modernization mean the material aspects of modernization which are different from the intangible cultural aspects of modernization.

One is tempted to think that a government that puts a high premium on man would not be so concerned with his material but not his medical welfare. What do material things mean to an unhealthy person?

There seems to be another divergence between the principles of humanism as espoused by President Kaunda and their application, especially in the field of education. We have already mentioned the monumental manpower problems that Zambia inherited at independence. We did not expect that these would be solved within just a mere decade. Even today, although Zambia has done a great deal to ease the situation, we see a new dependence on expatriate manpower in the field of education. For example, the 100 new secondary schools built after independence are still over 90 percent manned by expatriate teachers, which means, as Charles Harvey points out, that "teaching in these fields and other post-primary educational institutions is overwhelmingly in the hands of people new to Zambia and thus marginally adapted to Zambia's special needs."[29] Also, such a practice is especially at variance with the national objective to teach students the importance of collective effort "in the context of principles of Zambian Humanism."[30]

But in spite of these problems the Zambian figures for literacy are no doubt impressive, at least within the context of Africa. The percentage of illiterate population in the age group of 15 and over was 52.6 in 1970, which is quite remarkable when compared to 88.5 for Nigeria, 75.0 for Ghana, 80.0 for Kenya, 85.0 for Tanzania, 95.0 for Ethiopia, 73.7 for Egypt, and 81.2 for Algeria in the same year.[31]

CONCLUSION

In summary, is humanism working in Zambia? Zambia has achieved much since humanism was instituted as a development ideology. There has been a great improvement in education attainment as well as an increase in employment opportunities. The Zambians have almost successfully taken over the control of the economy, which was heavily in foreign hands. We have pointed out that Zambia's economy is nearly 90 percent dependent on copper mining, and that at independence the industry was owned and controlled by two South African and American companies that also had several links with other multinational mining and finance groups. However, independence coupled with the institution of the ideology of humanism as a development philosophy as well as the subsequent unilateral declaration of independence by Rhodesia gave Zambia an opportunity to protect her economy. Thus after the 1968 Mulungushi Conference* of Zambia's ruling party, new

*The Mulungushi Conference, held in April 1968, gave birth to the Mulungushi Declaration, an address by President Kaunda to the National Council of UNIP. The address outlines the economic program by which humanism would be implemented.

economic reforms were instituted. These resulted in Zambia taking over the copper companies and obtaining majority shares in some 26 other industrial companies.[32]

Zambian humanism has also made the Zambians fearless in exposing their weaknesses and difficulties in human relations, which in itself is good for the progress of development. One of the major drawbacks to progress is poor human relations, which usually lead to political strife. And political instability retards development.

Another advantage of humanism in Zambia is that the Zambians have come to realize that the basis of cooperation is self-help, self-reliance, hard work, and faithful participation by members in every cooperative society. These are also the essential qualities of good citizenship, whether in the local community or the nation at large.

The implementation of humanism has not been totally successful, and its application seems to result in some dilemmas. The government has run into the dilemma of maintaining a balance between man-centered as well as money-centered societies. President Kaunda bewailed this dilemma in his Mulungushi Declatation:

> Wealth like knowledge or any other instrument of service to man we think of, becomes an instrument of oppression and suppression if we do not handle it properly. . . . [But, he continues,] there is yet another field in which we must work hard. And this is generating interest in our people so that they can look at economic development of the country as the most important cornerstone of nation-building. One must add that once interest is generated we must work hard to keep it there.[33]

There is clearly a dilemma of trying to motivate interest in people to accumulate wealth and prevent them from using it to exploit their fellow men. To solve this dilemma the president declared: "Any form of exploitation of one man by another is to be fought in Zambia: we hope not only by this generation but also by generations to come."[34] He fails, however, to indicate how this fight will be carried on.

Not minding these problems of implementation, Zambian humanism seems to be well established even though it is still in the bud stage. But with proper care, nurture, and time it may bloom.

NOTES

1. K. D. Kaunda, Humanism in Zambia (Lusaka: Government Printer, 1967).
2. Ibid., p. 11.
3. Ibid., p. 12.
4. Ibid., p. 14.

5. For details, see ibid. Chapter 3.

6. K. Kaunda, Towards Complete Independence: After Mulungushi (Lusaka: Government Printer, 1969). The code is also quoted in Martin Minogue and Judith Molloy, eds., African Aims and Attitudes: Selected Documents (Cambridge University Press, 1974), p. 119.

7. Statistical and Economic Information Bulletin for Africa, no. 6 (1974), p. 59.

8. Ibid, p. 59.

9. This was an address to the National Council of UNIP, December 1, 1972.

10. Minogue and Molloy, op. cit., p. 128.

11. Eleazar Iwuji, "Report on Wage Salary Structures in English-Speaking Africa," in ILO/DANIDA Regional Seminar on Wages (Geneva: International Labor Office, 1974), p. 75.

12. For a complete elaboration of the human resource "problem profile," see Frederick H. Harbison, Human Resources as the Wealth of Nations (New York: Oxford University Press, 1973).

13. Iwuji, op. cit., p. 75.

14. Republic of Zambia, Manpower Report (Lusaka: Government Printer, 1966) pp. 1-2.

15. Zambia, Ministry of Education, Report on Education (Lusaka: Government Printer, August 1969).

16. Zambia, Second National Development Plan, 1972-1976 (Lusaka: Government Printer, 1971).

17. For details on Zambianization, see K. Kaunda, Zambia's Economic Revolution: The Mulungushi Declaration (Lusaka: Government Printer, 1968), and also Minogue and Molloy, op. cit., pp. 109-18.

18. See Charles Harvey, "The Structure of Zambian Development," in Development Paths in Africa and China, Ukandi G. Damachi et al. (London: Macmillian, 1970), Chapter 6.

19. For details see Mark Bostock and Charles Harvey, eds, Economic Independence and Zambian Copper (New York: Praeger, 1972).

20. Iwugi, op. cit., p. 77.

21. For details, see Zambia, Second National Development Plan, op. cit., p. 10.

22. Iwuji, op. cit., pp. 85-87.

23. Ibid., p. 77.

24. Ibid., p. 78.

25. Ibid., p. 78.

26. Ibid., p. 78.

27. African Annual Review, 1972 (London: Africa Journal Ltd.).

28. Ibid.

29. Harvey, "The Structure of Zambian Development," op. cit., p. 146.

30. Kaunda, Humanism in Zambia, op. cit., p. 24.

31. United Nations, Survey of Economic Conditions in Africa (New York: UN, 1972).

32. For details, see Kaunda, Zambia's Economic Revolution, op. cit.

33. Minogue and Molloy, op. cit., pp. 110-11.

34. Ibid., p. 111.

CHAPTER

3

HOUPHOUËT-BOIGNY: THE IVORY COAST—AN EXTENSION OF THE WEST

In order to understand the development ideology of Houphouët-Boigny, we need a short historical review of the country.

THE COUNTRY AND ITS HISTORY

The Ivory Coast obtained her independence from France in August 1960. In order to better appreciate the political and economic direction of the modern Ivory Coast, it is necessary to go back to 1893 when she first became a French colony. Of course, the history of French administration in West Africa, and particularly the role of the Ivory Coast, is so complex that it will suffice here to highlight only the most significant events and concepts.

From 1893 up to the time of the Ivory Coast's independence, French policy in her West African territories vacillated between the concepts of assimilation and association. The former advocated the universalist and egalitarian ideas of the French Revolution. It was opposed to slavery and colonial exploitation, asserting that all men are equal and thus should be treated alike.

The policy of association, on the other hand, in a Napoleonic arrogance, was blunt and direct in affirming the French as superiors and masters in the colonies.

However, a perceptive understanding of these two lofty concepts would reveal that they were essentially both one and the same or that, at least, they complemented each other. As actually practiced by successive French administrations and authorities, both in the metropolis and in the territories, the universalism so glowingly enshrined in the assimilationist concept was circumscribed by French language, French institutions, French laws, French customs. The credo of both concepts was the inherent superiority of the French culture over all others; the assimilationist concept so warmly advocated by the liberal, radical, and Communist intellectuals of the metropolis was nothing more than a comfortable shroud for the chauvinistic assertions of the incipient Gaullist. Yet the assimilationist concept had a soporific effect on many educated Africans who, for more than a half a century believing in eventual equality with Frenchmen of the metropolis, were not desirous of, and were even opposed to, complete independence from France.

France ruled the territories through executive decrees. In 1895 a presidential decree grouped all her West African territories to form what is called the General Government of West Africa (GGAO). France had insisted that the colonies must be economically self-supporting, but she soon realized it was impossible for some of them to pay their way. In 1904, in order to pool the resources of all the colonies, another presidential decree was issued that reconstituted the GGAO with a federation known as Afrique Occidentale Francaise (AOF) which was administered by a French governor-general resident in Dakar.

Having thus eliminated a potential burden on the colonial master, the next step was to make the colonies economically viable enough to yield profit. This was how French efforts at economic development in AOF began. As the Ivory Coast had become the richest of the AOF members, French economic activities were concentrated there. It was at that time that cash crops such as coffee and bananas, which today are the mainstay of Ivory Coast economy, were introduced by European farmers.

World War II was significant in determining the future of all AOF. France had fallen to the Germans and was being ruled by the German-allied Vichy government under Marshall Pétain. The AOF members were confronted with a choice of declaring their loyalty either to Marshall Pétain or to General de Gaulle, who had set up headquarters in London. The French government-general of the AOF declared his personal loyalty to Pétain but the Ivorians, considering the Vichy government a usuper, favored de Gaulle's Free French Movement and did everything to sabotage the Vichy war effort, mostly through agents in Ghana.

Under the Vichy government the AOF suffered terribly. Economic exploitation was accelerated through intensified forced labor and farmers were assigned quotas of foodstuff to help meet the needs of the German armies. Coupled with this was the unleashing of fierce Nazi racism against the Africans.

After the defeat of the Germans by the allies, a French provisional government was set up in Algiers. In 1944 a conference of the governors of AOF, North Africa, and Madagascar was called in Brazzaville to discuss the problems of the Africans and the new French Constitution that was to be allowed to send two delegates or deputies to the assembly in Paris and to be represented in other parliamentary forums. In 1945 the Ivory Coast elected Houphouët-Boigny as one of her deputies. His election later on helped to influence his ideology.

In 1946 the French Constitution establishing a French Union of Metropolitan France and her overseas territories was approved by the French assembly. While the deputies from North Africa and Madagascar, who were more radical in their views, had demanded independence, all the black African deputies, including Houphouët-Boigny, favored self-government within the framework of metropolitan France, a revival of the assimilationist concept.

In an ironic sense, cultural and political consciousness among black Africans of the AOF could be said to have begun during the Vichy era. For the first time, they were being told officially, and in blunt language, that the black man was inferior to the French man. After the collapse of the Vichy government, the Africans still extolled assimilationism but this time they began to wonder whether the equality of all men, French and African alike, was an obtainable goal within the framework of the French Union.

But more specifically, political agitation in the Ivory Coast actually began with economic and legal grievances. The first grievance the Ivorians had was against l'Inidigénat, a disciplinary penalty often inflicted by French administrative officers who presided over the native courts. The second was against forced labor, long practiced in the AOF but intensified during the Vichy government. We have indicated that between the two World Wars the Europeans has introduced cash crop farming into the Ivory Coast and that over the years a corps of wealthy African planters had mushroomed. Prominent among this group of planters was Houphouët-Boigny, who at the time was also a chief and a trained physician. However, colonial policy discriminated against the African planters, for it not only allowed the forced labor system to supply European planters with African workers but it also gave European planters, whose crops already commanded higher prices, access to protected markets. These colonial discriminatory practices led the Africans in 1944 to form the African Agricultural Union (Syndicat Agricole Africaine, SAA)--the first anti-colonial organization in the Ivory Coast. In 1946, the Democratic Party of the Ivory Coast (PDCI) was created out of the SAA to attract wider following than its predecessor which had been, essentially, a businessmen's organization. For a year or two the PDCI enjoyed the goodwill of the French Government in the Ivory Coast. But after 1947, when the colonial administration was replaced with a strongly conservative one, the PDCI came under constant harrassment because of its alliance, through the African Democratic Rally (RDA)--an interritorial organization of all the AOF political leaders—with the French Communist party. It should be pointed out that it was only the Communist party that had sided with the RDA in its campaign against the resurgence of conservative and colonialist feeling in metropolitan France. But with the political fortunes of the PDCI evaporating fast, in 1951 Houphouët-Boigny broke all ties with the Communist party and embarked on a policy of practical cooperation with the French union, later becoming one of its strongest advocates. This was another factor that contributed to the formulation of his ideology.

The emergence of Charles de Gaulle in 1958, and the dissolution of the Fourth Republic, marked another milestone in the Ivory Coast's road to independence. The Constitution was revised, creating the Fifth Republic, and effecting new changes in the relationship between France and the overseas territories. Most important, it put an end to the assimilationist illusion. Instead it provided for a free association of autonomous republics within the French community in which France was to be the senior partner. The community had jurisdiction over foreign policy, defense, currency, common ethnic and financial policy, policy on strategic raw materials, and over higher education, internal and external communications, and supervision of tribunals. No provision was made for eventual independence for members of the community. Again it has to be pointed out that the Ivory Coast, under the leadership of Houphouët-Boigny, voted almost unanimously in favor of the new Constitution. The main reason behind the Ivory Coast's vote was that although she was the wealthiest of the AOF, she felt she did not have the financial and manpower resources to develop independently of France. In other words, for the Ivory Coast and for Houphouët-Boigny the advantages of union with France were too significant to exchange for complete independence. Another lesser reason was the Ivory Coast, under the influence of anti-Federalist Houphouët-Boigny, had for long resented the revenue-sharing arrangement of the AOF. Now she thought that with the creation of the community, the AOF would finally be dissolved, paving the way for direct links between each self-governing colony and metropolitan France.

In 1959 the Ivory Coast obtained self-government. In the first elections for the new legislature the PDCI was elected and Houphouët-Boigny resigned his post with the French government to head the new government in the Ivory Coast. But a few months later Houphouët-Boigny had another grievance against France. Influenced by political events in Africa, the French government in early 1960 had sponsored an amendment to the 1958 Constitution that allowed members of the community to gain independence but to remain in the community that was reconstituted along Commonwealth lines. Houphouët-Boigny strongly opposed the reconstituted community and in August 1960 took the Ivory Coast from the community to become independent.[1]

We have given this historical summary of the Ivory Coast for very significant reasons. First, we have seen that throughout the period of French rule in the Ivory Coast, the latter never asked for independence but, instead, argued strongly for union with metropolitan France. Her decision to become independent in 1960 was an angry reaction to France's decision to loosen up the Union along Commonwealth lines. Second, Houphouët-Boigny is today one of the most controversial African leaders. His present pro-European image seems to derive from his assimilationist concept, which in turn is rooted in the history of French rule in the AOF. Third, it is believed that his leadership and development is still influenced by, if not essentially rooted in, that history. This history seems to place Houphouët-Boigny and the Ivory Coast in a different plane from that occupied by most other leaders and countries in Africa today.

"AN EXTENSION OF THE WEST"

We must point out that President Houphouët-Boigny, unlike the other African leaders with professed ideologies, has not formally declared an articulated ideology. He has made allusion to his ideas about development in speeches and writings. Nevertheless, we shall try to portray these ideas here as best we can.

As we pointed out, Houphouët-Boigny was himself a wealthy planter before independence and he believes that man is primarily an economic being. He was known to have appealed constantly to Ivorians to ignore Nkrumah's "political kingdom"—to him an unprofitable kingdom in terms of human needs—but instead to seek a life-sustaining kingdom based on coffee and cocoa production. "They fetch you a good price and you will become rich."[2]

In a review of his 1971-75 development plan he is also known to have told Ivorians that "now, it is not necessary to conceal that our development efforts lead toward . . . the Consumer Society (as it is known in the West)."[3] In 1959 he had stressed that his development goal was to make the Ivory Coast "an extension of the West."[4] Writing in Fraternité the following year (February 5, 1960), he expanded on the theme by rejecting solidarity with the Third World countries because they "cannot, given their present state of affairs, offer us anything other than the sharing of their own poverty."[5] From the preceding it is very clear that Houphouët-Boigny believes that economic prosperity in the Ivory Coast can come about only by total reliance on assistance from the West and by promotion of a Western-style free market economy. Accordingly, since independence, Houphouët-Boigny has scoffed any appeal to Africanize the economy; rather he has insisted that the colonial structure of the economy and labor force be kept intact since Africanization at this stage of development would be disruptive.[6] What is the impact of this strategy on the Ivory Coast's development?

PERFORMANCE OF ACTION PROGRAMS

Population

A short description of the population of the Ivory Coast is a necessary prerequisite for evaluating her development process. Between 1960 and 1972 the population had increased from 3.2 million to 4.5 million

The European population had also increased from 15,000 in 1960 to 40,000 in 1972.[7] The population growth rate increased from 2.8 percent between 1960 and 1965 to 3 percent between 1965 and 1969. This rate was the highest in francophone Africa. But during the period 1970-74 this rate declined to 2.7 percent because of a government comprehensive program on population control.[8]

Since 1960 the urban population has increased from 10.2 percent in 1960 to 19.0 percent in 1970. But the bulk of the population is still in the rural areas. The rural population decreased from 89.8 percent in 1960 to 81.0 percent by 1970. The growth rate of the urban population between 1965 and 1970 was 8.6 percent.[9] There are no available statistics for the 1971-75 period.

As previously pointed out, the Ivory Coast had been ruled not as the English-speaking West African countries were ruled, as a different people with a different culture who would one day aspire to be free, but as a province of France sharing a common, cultural heritage with France. The aim of France's assimilationist concept was not only to preach the gospel of French cultural supremacy, or just to bring the Ivorians into its civilizing influence, but also to make them accept it as the only culture in which the universality of men was entrenched, and in which Africans and Frenchmen were not only equal but one and the same.

The effects of this assumption were, of course, multifarious, but we will mention only the two more significant and apparent ones. First, since the Ivorians and their colonizers all were assumed to be French citizens, one people working for a common destiny, it was not necessary that jobs in the Ivory Coast be filled only by Ivorians per se, who, in any case, were regarded as French citizens of overseas provinces. The metropolitan French citizens had to be brought in to ensure that the economic and administrative machineries were in good hands and also to facilitate the civilizing mission. Second, since independence was out of the question and since metropolitan Frenchmen could always be brought to run the top segments of the government and economy, it was not necessary, or at least not urgent, that Ivorians be trained to assume responsibility in the Ivory Coast. As it has been observed by some writers, "the aim of French educational policy down to 1958 was very simple--namely to make. . . [Africans] worthy French citizens."[10] Thus when Houphouët-Boigny unexpectedly opted for independence in 1960, after ratifying the Union Constitution just in 1958, the Ivory Coast was ill-prepared in terms of educated manpower—a problem that still exists even today.

Education

To be more precise, not many Ivorians were given anything worth being called education until World War I. The school participation rate was said to be one of the worst both in Africa and in the world for not more than 5 out of every 100 children were exposed to any kind of formal education; even the few who were so lucky hardly went beyond the elementary level.

Between 1900 and 1946 the total number of primary school graduates was below 15,000. It has also been suggested that the low participation rate was partly because of the Ivorians' reluctance to submit to French education. The schools were, in fact, later referred to as "schools for the sons of chiefs." This belief is well demonstrated by Yambo Oulouguem in his famous novel, Bound to Violence.[11] Although a few vocational schools existed, until 1945 there were only two secondary schools in the whole of AOF (the Lycée Faidherbe and the Ecole William Ponty), both of which were located in Senegal. The Ecole William Ponty was the highest level to which most post primary students could aspire. It trained a few teachers and prepared a few students for entry into the Dakar "Medical School" who could, on completion, become "Medicins africains" or assistant doctors. But even then the number of graduates from William Ponty between 1918 and 1945, that is for the whole of AOF, was less than 2,000. It is this small group that formed the intellectual and political elite of the AOF. It should be noted that President Houphouët-Boigny was a graduate of William Ponty. By 1945, the Ivory Coast had less than 12 university graduates.

However, political reforms in metropolitan France affected the educational system in the Ivory Coast, as in all other AOF countries. More money was directed to education and by 1957 the number of pupils enrolled in primary school in the Ivory Coast had reached 126,000, about five times the enrolment in 1948; secondary school enrolment jumped to 4,300; and the number of university students zoomed to 1,130. But again the anomaly in this last figure is that it includes both Ivorians and Europeans. Although enrolment in primary and secondary levels had increased, not more than 25 percent of the primary-school-age population went to school and about 1 percent of the secondary-school-age were in school. These figures compare rather unfavorably with those in Nigeria, which also got independence in 1960 and of Ghana, whose independence was in 1957. By 1960 the figures for the Ivory Coast were 239,000 primary (Ghana 477,000), 11,4000 secondary (Ghana 15,100). The figures for Ghana exclude enrolments in private nonassisted primary and secondary schools. Between 1954 and 1957 while secondary enrolment rose to 77 percent in Nigeria and 114 percent in Zambia, it was only 23 percent in all of the AOF. Yet it is to be remarked that in 1954 only 500 junior secondary schools (that is, four years postprimary) and fewer than 150 full secondary school certificates were awarded in Senegal, Guinea, and the Ivory Coast. Thus it is estimated that although the secondary enrolment increased substantially, not more than 1000 secondary school graduates were being produced in the Ivory Coast until the 1960s.[12]

At independence educational expansion in the Ivory Coast was great. By December 1960 there were 1,722 primary schools with a total enrolment of 239,000. In 1963 between 45 percent and 50 percent of primary-school-age children were in school and the secondary school enrolment ratio was 4:1. By 1963-64, the Ivory Coast was spending 5.3 percent of her national income on education, which is very high indeed. Vocational education had also been expanded and by 1962 there were 20 institutions. In the same year about 400 Ivorians were studying in technical institutes in France, Senegal, or Mali. In 1963, 1,400 Ivorian students were studying in France and 1,000 were in local institutions attached to the Abidjan Center of Higher Studies, which had been established in 1959, and a few were at the University of Dakar.[13] To give us a more realistic picture of what educational development was at independence, let us compare school enrolment in the Ivory Coast with that of her neighboring country Ghana (see Table 3.1). In 1965, the population of Ghana was almost 8 million while that of the Ivory Coast was 3.9 million.

TABLE 3.1

School Enrolment in the Ivory Coast and Ghana, 1965-66

Level	Ivory Coast	Ghana
Primary	353,700	1,137,500
Secondary	28,100	312,700
Technical	3,800	6,700
Higher	1,900	4,300

Source: Philip J. Foster and Aristide R. Zolberg, Ghana and the Ivory Coast (Chicago: University of Chicago Press, 1971), p. 273.

It is unfortunate that more recent statistics are not available, but we can make a few observations and assumptions. The first observation is that before independence the educational system in the Ivory Coast had been grossly inadequate, which explains her low school enrolment figures. We have previously given reasons for this situation. The second observation is that shortly before independence great efforts had been made to expand the system rapidly. After independence the efforts have continued but not as great as to the point of providing the much-needed indigenous high manpower. Third, adult or mass education has been scant. Fourth, at least until 1967, the educational system has changed very little from its colonial structure. On the whole, the Ivory Coast has embarked on educational expansion and is beginning to produce a good corps of educated Ivorians to assume positions of responsibility.

Labor Force and Employment

What is the impact of this educational expansion on the Ivory Coast's labor force and employment? We have indicated that before independence, of all the members of AOF, the Ivory Coast was the wealthiest because it was there that the Europeans had first introduced the cultivation of export crops such as coffee and bananas. This had also led to the concentration of French economic activities that were related to the agricultural industry. It was estimated that in 1962 about 90 percent of the labor force was engaged in agricultural and related activities —working either on small family holdings or on huge plantations. In 1970 it was estimated that 81 percent of the total labor force of 1.2 million was probably engaged in agriculture and related activities.[14]

The agricultural sector is overwhelmingly foreign. Although over the years a sizable corps of African planters mushroomed, the large farms and plantations were, and are still, owned by Europeans, mainly French. But the laborers who work in them, because of the ordinary Ivorian's aversion to manual labor, are Africans from neighboring states, especially Upper Volta, Mali, Guinea, and Ghana. However, of the 81 percent engaged in agriculture in 1970, 22 percent (270,000) were in wage employment. Table 3.2 gives us the occupational breakdown of wage employment in 1962 (the year that statistics are available).

TABLE 3.2

Occupational Breakdown of Wage Employment in the Ivory Coast, 1962

Labor Force	Ivorians	Non-Ivorian Africans	Europeans	Total
Managers	230	54	1,280	1,560
Professional and technical	540	92	2,100	2,700
Supervisory (foremen)	860	217	1,670	2,750
Skilled clerical	190	580	1,180	4,940
Skilled manual	6,800	2,300	140	9,200
Semiskilled clerical	8,000	3,000	310	11,300
Semiskilled manual	11,200	4,200	40	15,400
Unskilled laborers	18,700	34,.600	100	53,300
Apprentices	1,100	440	20	1,580
Total	50,000	45,483	6,800	102,983

Source: Frederick Harbison and Charles Myers, Manpower and Education (New York: McGraw-Hill, 1965), p. 247.

These statistics show that in 1962 the number of foreigners in the salaried labor force exceeded that of Ivorians, but that the majority of foreign Africans were employed as laborers, mainly on the farms and plantations. The two top categories and the next two middle levels were overwhelmingly Europeans. Europeans made up about 82 percent of the managers, professionals, and technicians, Ivorians about 15 percent, and non-Ivorian Africans 3 percent. It was only in the low middle level of the labor force that Ivorians dominated. By 1965 the statistics had worsened for the Ivorians. The percentage of Europeans in the Managerial level had increased to about 87 percent and in the technical category to 85 percent. That means that the percentage of Ivorians had declined to 9.8 percent while that of non-Ivorians stood at about 3.5 percent. For the Foreman category, Europeans now stood at 57 percent while the Ivorians had increased rapidly to 32 percent. But the figures for 1967 had deteriorated further. Europeans controlled 91.3 percent of the Managerial level and had only declined to their 1964 figure of 81.7 percent for the Technical category, and 54 percent of the Foreman.[15] And by 1969 they formed 93.6 percent of Managerial and Senior staff.[16]

Two observations could be made from these statistics: First, the private sector has maintained a quick and steady growth from 1962, when the total labor force of this sector was 103,000, to 1967 with the figure of 129,684. Second, as the sector expanded Ivorians were coming more and more into the middle categories as the Europeans increased their control at top levels. This perhaps reflects Houphouët-Boigny's policy of dependence on Western assistance. As the economy grows and expands, and more visions of prosperity are had, there is more and more dependence on that assistance. Another possible reason for this statistical phenomenon could be that economic growth outstripped the educational system and as a result more foreigners, especially Europeans, had to be hired. But this is not to say that Europeans, especially the French, are confined to top-level jobs. As Table 3.2 has indicated, the French are to be found in the lower categories of the economy as well. They work as truck drivers, clerks, secretaries, and as salesclerks in all major sales departments. In fact, European women are preferred to Ivorian women as clerks and secretaries and it is said that almost all salesclerks in Abidjan are the wives and daughters of European technicians, military personnel, and administrators.[17] It is therefore not surprising that women constitute 28 percent of the European wage earners. But the Ivorian women make up only 2 percent of the African salaried labor force. Maybe Houphouët-Boigny's concept of man as an "economic being" or "homo economicus" does not extend to Ivorian women.

It is estimated that between 1960 and 1966 the population of foreign Africans and Europeans in the labor force grew by 40 percent and 35 percent, respectively, while that of Ivorians increased by only

16 percent.[18] Foreign control of the labor force is not only in the private sector, but also in the public sector. While the Ivorians occupy higher-level positions in the public sector than in the private and are more in number here, overwhelming non-Ivorian Africans by more than four to one, the Europeans still control the top segment of many strategic government departments, which is in line with the national ideology of making the Ivory Coast an extension of the West.

Nevertheless, Houphouët-Boigny has begun to aim at Ivorization, even though this is being done at an extremely slow pace. He is determined to avoid acceleration of the process unless there are qualified Ivorians who are as competent as the Europeans.

Little wonder then that there is an acute shortage of indigenous high-level manpower. Although independent for 15 years now, the Ivory Coast still relies very heavily on skilled manpower from France. Houphouët-Boigny has insisted on not speeding the Ivorization process at the expense of efficiency; that is, until there are qualified Ivorians to replace Frenchmen. What are the possible implications of such a policy? First, the education planners are so thoroughly French and traditional and the educational and economic institutions are so thoroughly staffed by Frenchmen that is is going to take many years before the ordinary Ivorian would be given the opportunity to acquire the needed experience that Houphouët-Boigny demands. Moreover, his insistence on educational qualification and competence may not be taken too seriously since the presence of Europeans is felt not only in the echelons of government and industry but also in low-middle levels of commerce. Thus, it is significant to note that his Ivorization policy does not involve dismantling of the colonial structure but, rather, a quiet superimposition on it. It becomes questionable whether the Ivorians would ever become "economic men" — what Houphouët-Boigny's ideology purports to make them. We may then ask to what extent does the Ivorian benefit from the fruits of Ivory Coast's development?

Economic Development

As we have pointed out earlier, Houphouët-Boigny, unlike other African leaders, is a self-confessed, unabashed entrepreneur of the free-enterprise mold. His development goal has been to make the Ivory Coast an extension of the West, a consumer society, and to make the ordinary Ivorian rich. We have also pointed out that of all the AOF during French rule, the Ivory Coast was the wealthiest, depending on her diversified export crop farming. To a very large extent, through the guidance of Houphouët-Boigny, the Ivory Coast has prospered, although the economy is still appallingly foreign-controlled.

In 1960 the GDP was about CFAF 125 billion ($500 million).*

*CFAF means Communauté Financière Africaine Franc.

Agriculture contributed 52 percent of domestic product and 92 percent of exports. Commerce share was 32 percent; transport and communications 5 percent; industry and construction 4 percent each; forestry 2 percent.[19] It was estimated that although the industrial production was still insignificant, its growth rate between 1957 and 1960 was 21 percent but overall economic growth was 37 percent. In 1962 the government master plan for economic development into the 1970s aimed at raising the annual per capita of the Ivorian from the 1960 figure of CFAF 34,500 ($138) to at least CFAF 125,000 ($500) and also to put an end to foreign aid. Up until then the Ivory Coast was one of the most aided countries in the world, receiving about $50 million annually from France and the European Economic Community countries (EEC).[20] How has the country fared according to the plan? The Ivory Coast's economic growth during the plan period (1963-72) was outstanding by worldwide comparison. In 1965 the gross domestic product (GDP) had grown from the 1960 figure of CFAF 125 million to CFAF 223 billion, and the following year to CFAF 242 billion. Between 1960 and 1965 the average annual rate of growth was about 11 percent (at market prices) or 8 percent (at constant prices). By 1966, too, the overall industrial output had climbed from CFAF 12.7 billion in 1960 to CFAF 51.4 billion in 1966, a more than fourfold increase.[21]

In spite of the high population growth rate of 3.0, the per capita income had also shot up. Thus by 1966 the per capita GDP too had jumped from CFAF 34,500 in 1960 to CFAF 44,750. By 1968 the GDP had registered CFAF 248.4 billion and per capita GDP stood at CFAF 52,136. From 1960 to 1966 the average annual growth rate was still about 11 percent (at constant prices). The industrial sector had also increased to CFAF 62.4 billion, about 19 percent of total GDP, a phenomenal increase from the 4 percent figure in 1960.[22]

In 1969 the GDP had reached $1.31 billion; by 1970 it was $1.49 billion; and in 1971 it stood at $1.53 billion. Similarly, by 1969 the per capita GDP had climbed to $311, in 1970, it was $346 and in 1971, $346, thus giving the Ivory Coast one of the highest per capita GDP in all Africa in 1971. The average per capita GDP for Africa as a whole was $167 in 1971 and for West Africa it was $250.[23]

There is no doubt that under Houphouët-Boigny, the Ivory Coast has prospered. But this rapid economic growth has been criticized for a number of reasons. Some critics have characterized it as growth without development, meaning that, notwithstanding the increase in production and income, the economy is still dominated by foreigners, chiefly Frenchmen. Others wonder whether the prosperity has been shared evenly among the population.

Wage differential figures are not available for Ivorians and expatriates but there are figures for levels of occupation and for urban and rural. It has often been said that Abidjan is a showcase for the whole country, even that Abidjan is the Ivory Coast. To some extent these statements are true. In 1961 it was calculated that the average annual wage was above CFAF 298,400 ($1,193), one of the highest in all of Africa and about nine times higher than the per capita income. The wage structure in 1962 was broken down as shown in Table 3.3 while that of 1968-69 is shown in Table 3.4.

TABLE 3.3

The Wage Structure in the Ivory Coast, 1962

Category of Employment	Average Monthly Wages (in CFA francs)
Technician, foreman, manager	62,940.82
Semiskilled worker (2)	9,473.40
Semiskilled worker (1)	9,028.80
Skilled worker (1)	10,909.80
Skilled worker (2)	11,662.20
Unskilled worker	7,113.60

Source: T. D. Roberts, Area Handbook for Ivory Coast, 2d ed. (Washington, D.C.: U. S. Department of the Army, 1973), pp. 341-42.

TABLE 3.4

Distribution of Work Force and Wages in the Secondary Sector by Skills and Origin in the Ivory Coast, 1968-69

Category	Percent of Total Labor Force	Percent of Total Wages Paid
Skill level		
Managerial and senior staff	1.6	18.2
Foreman	4.5	21.4
Skilled workers	14.5	18.4
Unskilled workers	79.4	42.0
Total	100.0	100.0

Source: International Labor Office, Employment in Africa: Some Critical Issues (Geneva: ILO, 1971), p. 196.

These statistics show that the top one-twentieth of the labor force received more than one-third of the total wages paid. A further breakdown would have revealed that in 1967, 89.7 percent of all Ivorians in the modern sector of the economy occupied the bottom half of the labor force and that in government service they formed only 13 to 15 percent of the top ranks. We, however, assume that the Ivorian percentages may have improved since 1967, although we do not expect spectacular changes.

In the Ivory Coast wage imbalances not only occur between levels of skills or occupations, but also between locations and sectors. For example, in 1965, whereas the monetary income in the Northern region of the country was CFAF 5,400 per capita, in the Center region it was CFAF 37,500, and in Abidjan it was as high as CFAF 201,000. Even within the same regions the differentials are great. For instance, in the Northern region (1965) while per capita income in the rural area was CFAF 3,000 in the urban it was CFAF 52,000. In 1961 a farming family's annual income was $140 or CFAF 35,000; that of a cocoa- or coffee-growing family was $240 or CFAF 60,000; but that of a wage earner was $1,213 or CFAF 298,400.[24]

Social Development

From the figures above we can see that income distribution is very uneven in the Ivory Coast; but that does not seem to worry Houphouët-Boigny, who is more concerned with creating economic opportunities for his people (to put it in his words) to enable them to "get rich." Implicit in such an attitude is the principle of the "survival of the fittest" which connotes acute competition. The implication is that the Ivory Coast is presumably a competitive and not an ascriptive society where little attention is paid to social welfare.

Such inattention is markedly noticed in the area of health. In spite of the so-called prosperity in the Ivory Coast under Houphouët-Boigny, the country still has one of the highest infant mortality rates (138 per 1,000 births) and life expectancy is still only 41 years. That is, of course, not to say there has not been improvement in health facilities since independence, but the improvement has been marginal.

In 1961-62 there were about 3 large hospitals, 6 secondary hospitals, 54 medical centers, and 112 dispensaries. In 1961 there was a total of 6,500 hospital beds — about 1 for every 500 persons. In the same period there were 128 physicians working for the government (half of whom were French), 10 pharmacists (more than half French), 5 dentists, 85 midwives, and 1,280 nurses. In private practice there were 30 physicians, 30 pharmacists, 7 midwives, and 280 nurses, most of whom were French. This worked out at 1 physician for every 25,000 inhabitants and 1 nurse for 2,300 inhabitants. There is indeed a shortage of doctors, pharmacists, and especially the paramedical professionals. The dominance of foreigners in this area also seem worrying, particularly because they could leave at any time for one reason or another. Since there is no indigenous manpower readily available to replace them, a crisis may easily be created by their departure.

It is because of such uncertainties that the government is not only trying to train indigenous manpower but also to improve the facilities. As from 1972, the situation has changed, although not spectacularly. In 1972 there were 8 large hospitals (3 in Abidjan), 47 district hospitals, 169 dispensaries, 38 maternity centers, and 10 leprosy clinics. The personnel had risen to 218 physicians, 49 medical technicians, 108 midwives, and 1,372 nurses. The number of inhabitants per 1 doctor was 19,000. This ratio is not impressive when compared to that of the People's Republic of the Congo (1 doctor per 11,000 inhabitants), whose history is similar to and whose economic growth has not been as staggering as that of the Ivory Coast.

With regard to the consumption of durable goods, the figures are also not exceedingly impressive given the phenomenal economic performance of the Ivory Coast since her independence. In 1948 the total number of vehicles registered was 4,000. By 1961 there were 27,993, nearly evenly broken between cars and trucks.[25] In 1972 there were 50,000 cars, 29,800 commercial vehicles, 222,280 telephones, 65,000 radios, 6,500 television sets, 48 cinemas, and power consumption per head was 151 kilograms. If these figures are compared with those of Zambia, whose economic performance is similar to that of the Ivory Coast, it would be observed that the consumptive capacity of the Ivory Coast is less than that of Zambia.[26] It should be noted here that the basic tenet of Houphouët-Boigny's development ideology is to make the Ivory Coast a "consumer society." His professed ideology seems to be at variance with what actually obtains in the Ivory Coast.

This variance does not imply total failure. We have seen the social and economic statistics. Whereas the social aspect of the Ivory Coast cannot be said to be extraordinarily impressive, except perhaps for Abidjan, the economic aspect has been quite spectacular. It has been argued that this development could not have been possible without Houphouët-Boigny's policy of heavy reliance on Western assistance and personnel. It is also argued that this reliance and the dependence on export crops may have a limit. Export crops are subject to the vagaries of the world market and overreliance on foreigh personnel could drain financial resources as it will entail more and more remittances abroad. It is also questionable whether a country can really develop from the charity of others. But whether Houphouët-Boigny's magic wand could continue to be effective for many years to come is highly unpredictable. The magic wand has so far failed in one aspect — the Ivorians are still far from being "homines economici."

NOTES

1. T. D. Roberts, Area Handbook for Ivory Coast, 2d ed. (Washington, D.C.: U. S. Department of the Army, 1973).

2. M. F. Lofchie, The State of the Nations: Constraints on Development in Independent Africa (Berkeley: University of California Press, 1971), p. 122.

3. Ibid.

4. Ibid., p. 123.

5. Ibid.

6. Guy de Lusignan, French-Speaking Africa Since Independence (London: Pall Mall Press, 1969), pp. 137-38.

7. United Nations, Statistical Yearbook (Part 2) 1973 (New York: UN, 1973), pp. 1-11.

8. Roberts, op. cit., pp. xv-xvi.

9. Ibid., p. xvi.

10. Frederick H. Harbison and Charles Myers, Education, Manpower, and Economic Growth (New York: McGraw-Hill, 1964), pp. 235-38.

11. Yambo Oulouguem, Bound to Violence (New York: Harcourt, Brace, Jovanovitch, 1971).

12. Harbison and Myers, op. cit., pp. 241-42.

13. Ibid., pp. 265-66.

14. Roberts, op. cit., p. xviii.

15. International Monetary Fund, Surveys of African Economies, Vol. 3 (Washington, D.C.: IMF, 1970), p. 261.

16. International Labor Office, Employment in Africa: Some Critical Issues (Geneva: ILO, 1971), p. 196.

17. Roberts, op. cit., pp. 337-38.

18. Ibid., p. 338.

19. Lusignan, op. cit., p. 141. Also see Roberts, op. cit., pp. xliii-lvi.

20. Lusignan, op. cit., p. 142.

21. Ibid.

22. IMF, Surveys of African Economies, Vol. 3, op. cit., pp. 222-24.

23. United Nations, Survey of Economic Conditions in Africa, op. cit., pp. 47-49.

24. Roberts, op. cit., p. 157.

25. Ibid., p. 316.

26. See Chapter 2 for the figures on Zambia.

CHAPTER

4

SERETSE KHAMA: KAGISANO—A POLICY FOR HARMONY IN BOTSWANA

Sir Seretse Khama was born July 1, 1921 at Serowe. He is the grandson of Khama III, chieftain of the Bamangwato for 50 years until his death in 1923, and succeeded to the chieftainship at the age of four when his father died in 1925.

Khama was educated at home until the age of 10 when he was sent to South Africa to continue his education. He later entered Fort Hare University and graduated with a B.A. in history. Instead of taking up his chieftain's duties, he went to England to continue his studies, first at Balliol College, Oxford, then at Middle Temple, London.

A bitter political storm was provoked by his marriage on September 28, 1948, to Ruth Williams, a secretary at Lloyds Insurance Underwriters. The tribal leaders urged Khama to give up his wife, but he refused and returned home in a bid to persuade them to accept multiracial harmony. This controversy led the British government to ban him as a chief for not less than five years, and he was eventually deported.

The first step back to power came in October 1957 when Khama was chosen as one of the 25 members of the Tribal Council. On June 20, 1961 he was sworn in as leading African delegate to the Legislative Council. On January 29, 1962, he launched the Bechuanaland Democratic Party (BDP). Campaigning on a multiracial platform the BDG won 28 of the 31 seats in the new Legislative Assembly at the elections on March 2, 1965. Khama was appointed the first prime minister, and minister of home affairs, on March 3, 1965. A knighthood was conferred on him at independence on September 30, 1966, when he became president of the Republic of Botswana.

THE COUNTRY AND ITS HISTORY

Botswana, formerly Bechuanaland, became a British protectorate in 1891 and obtained its independence only in 1966. Its geographical location--it is flanked by South Africa in the south. Zambia in the north, Southwest Africa (Namibia) in the west, and Rhodesia in the east--gives it a political significance that may be argued to be well out of proportion to the strength of its population and its natural resources. Perhaps, too, its geographical position is responsible for its painful history.

When the former South African colonies of Transvaal, Orange Free State, the Cape, and Natal met in Durban in 1910 to consider proposals for a federation or union, the participants generally assumed that the Act of Union should make provision for the inclusion of the three high commission territories of Botswana, Lesotho, and Swaziland, which were then being administered by the Imperial government through a high commissioner stationed in South Africa (the colonies). Although the three successfully lobbied the British government against a transfer into a South African Union, the official British view at the time was in favor of a transfer and it was generally assumed it would only be a matter of time before this would take place. In fact in 1910 the British high commissioner informed the Botswana chiefs that his government could not say how long it would be before Botswana was handed over to the South African Union, adding cryptically that "in the natural course of things, this would take place some day."[1]

Britain had been loath to exercise any formal authority over Botswana; only some external factors--especially the desire to control the South African pipeline to the northern territories and the general frenzy of other colonial powers, namely Germany, in acquiring spheres of economic and political influence--finally compelled the Imperial government to act. Even then it acted with a light touch. Unlike in other British colonies in East and West Africa, there was hardly any form of administration beyond the maintenance of law and order. The protectorate was left to fend for itself, being asked to rely on revenue from its own resources for its development. Two reasons seemed to have been responsible for this attitude: The first is that Botswana was a poor territory, lacking in any appreciable natural resources and as such, except as a road to the interior, it was of little economic significance to the Imperial government. Second, for the British, still under the assumption that it was only a matter of time before Botswana could become part of the South African Union, the rationale was: "Why spend British taxpayers' money to build up a territory someone else is going to take over?"[2]

It was not until the early 1930s when the hope of incorporating the territory into the South African Union had vanished that the British Government decided to infuse some money into the financial blood of Botswana and to accept its colonial responsibility.

This brief summary of the history of Botswana and its former relationship with Britain and South Africa helps to explain the development problems of modern Botswana before and after independence. It also helps us to understand why President Khama has formulated his ideology of "Kagisano."

KAGISANO

The ideals enshrined in the ideology of "Kagisano" are unity, peace, harmony, and a sense of community. But for these ideals to be achieved, four national principles rooted in Botswana's past traditions and culture have been developed: "Puso ya batho ka batho" (democracy); "ditiro tsa ditlhabololo" (development); "boipelego" (self-reliance); and "popagano ya sechaba" (unity). President Khama fails to define each of these principles in his ideology, but the basic national objectives set by his government tend to provide adequate meaning for each of them:

1. Rapid Economic Growth: this should lead to a marked improvement in social welfare which is essential to maintain a sound basis for democracy and for preserving national unity and social harmony.
2. Social Justice: this gives rise to detailed policies concerning, for example, taxation, bursaries, land tenure and rural and regional development aimed at achieving a more equitable distribution of income and wealth, equal access to education and to the means for production, and hence equality of opportunity for self-advancement.
3. Economic Independence: this determines Botswana's policies concerning the diversification of the country's external economic and trade relations, the strengthening of internal production and the progressive localization of ownership, management and the labour force.
4. Sustained Production: this necessitates the careful conservation of agricultural and wildlife resources and the protection of the natural environment.[3]

From these objectives one thing becomes clear: Botswana's economy has to be a mixed one giving enough room for both government participation and private ownership. Although the ideology provides due consideration for social welfare of the citizens, it warns that "no one should think that the living standards of all the population can be raised by redistributing the assets of the few people who are relatively well-off, though such people must be prepared for sacrifices."[4]

On the whole, to maintain Kagisano, every Batswana must understand that Botswana is a poor country and, as a result, he should be prepared for hard work. Such determination and commitment on the part of the citizens will enable them to utilize the national resources-- men, money, minerals, the land--to promote development for their benefit. But how are the basic national objectives to be attained?

PROGRAM OF ACTION

The government is to pursue actively interventionist economic and social policies. The intervention is not to stifle private initiative, but rather to promote and guide it by creating favorable conditions. Besides, the government is determined to accelerate the training of the national labor force to augment the supply of skilled manpower, which is a prerequisite for expanding production. The highest priorities are given to:

1. expanding job opportunities, in particular by the creation of new industries;
2. expanding agricultural production on sustained basis, particularly with a view to increasing cash incomes in the rural areas;
3. improving living conditions in the rural areas. [5]

Although Botswana is faced with an acute shortage of capital resources and skilled manpower, she is determined to utilize the few natural resources she has to set a sound basis for long-term economic development. A two-pronged economic strategy has been adopted:

(a) securing rapid and large returns to the nation from intensive capital investment and mining and other viable modern industries mainly aimed at export markets; and
(b) re-investing the revenue from these investments in (i) education and training, (ii) the promotion of agriculture and labor-intensive manufacturing activities, and (iii) the improvement of services in the rural areas. [6]

To carry out such improvement there is a program for rural development that aims to achieve: (1) increased sustained production from the land and wildlife through research coordinated extension work and conservation planning leading to the introduction of correct land use and management practices; (2) improved marketing and credit facilities in the rural areas; (3) creation of new employment opportunities, especially promoting industries, services, and crafts wherever feasible and thereby reducing the numbers at present without any means of support; and (4) improved social services such as water supplies, education, medical and welfare services in the rural areas. [7] How successfully has this program of action been implemented?

EVALUATION OF DEVELOPMENT PERFORMANCE

Population

A general description of the population features of Botswana will provide a basic framework for understanding her development trend. It should be pointed out that because of her painful colonial history, there are few or no statistics on Botswana before 1964. The total resident population in 1964 was as shown in Table 4.1. It was estimated that about 55 percent of the population was less than 20 years of age. In 1969 the population had risen to 630,000 and by 1972 it stood at 690,000. The average annual growth rate between 1960 and 1970 was 3.1 percent,[8] which is quite high by UN standards.

TABLE 4.1

Resident Population in Botswana, 1964

Race	Population
Africans	535,000
Europeans	4,000
Colored*	3,500
Asians	500
Total	543,000

*In Botswana's parlance, "colored" are mulattoes.

Source: R. E. Culbertson, Senior Seminar in Foreign Policy: Bechuanaland--Resources for Nationhood and Development, mimeographed (Washington, D.C.: Foreign Services Institute, 1966), p. 3.

The bulk of the population lives in the rural areas (as Table 4.2 indicates). The urban sector is relatively small, even though there has been progressive increases with time.

TABLE 4.2

Percentage of Urban-Rural Population in Botswana, 1964, 1970, and 1971

Area	1964	1970	1971
Urban	3.2	6.8	8.6
Rural	96.8	93.2	91.4

Source: United Nations, Statistical Yearbook (Part 3) 1973 (New York: UN, 1973), p. 21.

With regard to the labor force, out of a total of 540,000 in 1964, the number of the economically active was 251,000. Of these the number in the agricultural sector was 228,000 or 90.8 percent, which was the same as that of Tanzania in 1967.

Education

As in most other African countries the dearth of skilled manpower in Botswana has always been one of the major obstacles to development. We have pointed out that the British government before the 1930s had been reluctant to give any developmental committment to Botswana and that even after that time its involvement was mostly in maintaining skeletal services. The initiative to establish schools for the benefit of the African population—notably the development of a unified educational system in the tribal areas—was taken by private groups such as missionary organizations. Hence in 1955, 166 primary schools existed in the country. This gradually rose to 241 in 1966 with a total enrolment of 62,000. Even most of these schools are said to have been so poor in basic facilities that they hardly deserved the name "institution." For example, it is said that more than 80 percent of the schools had no water supply; 80 percent had no latrines; about 50 percent of the pupils sat on desks in classrooms, another 15 percent sat on the floor because they had no desks, and the remaining 35 percent sat under trees on the ground.[9]

Until 1944 there was no secondary school in Botswana; the few Batswana who cared enough went to study in South Africa. However, in 1955 there were 4 secondary schools with an enrolment of 242 pupils, rising to eight with an overflowing enrolment of 1,036 in 1966. Teacher training and technical colleges rose from two with an enrolment of 75 to four with 400 students. In 1962 only five Batswana were enroled at the University of Botswana, Lesotho and Swaziland, then located in Lesotho. In the same year the total number of Batswana within the country who held B.A. degrees was 35.[10]

Since then, however, more Batswana have been awarded scholarships to study abroad. It is estimated that about 48 Batswana were studying in foreign universities by 1964 and that on the eve of independence there were some 90 Botswana university graduates, 581 secondary school graduates, 2,499 with "junior certificates" (that is, with three years of secondary education), and about 10,000 primary school certificate holders. The annual rate of production as of 1964 was 17 university graduates, 27 secondary school graduates, 136 secondary IV certificate holders, and 36 teachers.[11]

Since independence in 1966 much effort has been made to accelerate the production of qualified Batswana. Thus, the number of secondary schools had risen from 8 in 1966, to 10 in 1969, to 15 in 1973 (excluding private unaided ones), with a total enrolment of 6,152.[12] Technical and vocational schools had jumped from 1 trade school and 1 homecraft school in 1965 to 16 vocational schools in 1975 and 25 homecraft schools in 1973, with a total enrolment of 1,521 pupils. All this educational improvement was in keeping with the government policy of promoting rapid economic growth and independence.

Nevertheless, in 1964 it had been estimated that if the country's educational system maintained its annual rate of pupil turnout, that is, 17 university graduates, 27 high-school graduates, 136 Form IV certificate holders, and 36 teachers, it would take Botswana 10 years to meet the static demand of 1965, which was 2,291.[13] More effort is needed on the part of the government to meet the shortage of educated manpower.

Labor Force and Employment

Such shortage had direct impact on the labor force participation in the country. In 1964 the educational system could produce only 216 persons for an estimated 2,291 jobs, excluding the more general educational needs. Contrary to the objective of economic independence, the result was that the Botswana economy, both in the public and private sectors, was (and still is) dominated by expatriates. For example, in 1964, while the country could count only 90 Botswana degree holders, there were 310 expatriate university graduates, mostly South Africans, who held jobs in the country. Although there were 581 Botswana secondary school graduates, there were 873 expatriates. Thus out of 182 professional and administrative posts, only 21 were occupied by Batswana. In the lower category of executive and technical positions, out of 535 vacancies, only 114 were filled by local officers. And of the 61 teachers in the eight secondary schools only six were native Batswana.[14]

Two years after independence things had only improved slightly from their 1964 levels. In 1968 the number of employed non-Batswana was 2,803, which was 10 percent of the total persons employed in Botswana. Table 4.3 demonstrates the level of non-Batswana participation in the labor force.

Most of the key sectors of the economy were in foreign hands—for example, the financial institutions were totally dominated by foreigners. And such foreign dominance directly contravenes the national policy of economic independence.

Even the 1973 figures still show the foreign control of the economy. About 24 percent of the officers in the public service were expatriates; and in the senior administrative, professional, scientific, and technical fields the percentages of expatriates were 80 percent, 60 percent, 92 percent, and 83 percent, respectively. However, the figure of 683 expatriates in the civil service as of 1964 had dwindled to only 567 in 1968. Thus, although after independence many Batswana were employed in the newly created posts in the civil service, the relative ratio of

TABLE 4.3

Non-Batswana Participation in the Labor Force, 1968

Sector	Percentage
All financial institutions	53.7
Electricity and water	25.1
Services	24.7
Communications	18.7
Construction	13.5
Public administration	9.5
Manufacturing	8.5
Trade and hotels	7.2
Extractive industries	2.7

Source: Botswana, Ministry of Finance and Development Planning, Manpower and Employment in Botswana (Gaborone: Government Printer, 1973).

Batswana to expatriates did not alter much. The latter still dominated such important departments as finance, public works, transport and communications, and agriculture. Such control of the economy would have made sense if the Batswana were trained to take over gradually.

To stress the acuteness of the indigenous high-level manpower shortage in Botswana we present Table 4.4 on labor demand and supply as of August 1972. Again, expatriates filled practically all the vacancies that existed. Some departments, for example, Tsetse, Animal Health and Production, Land Utilization, are controlled completely by foreigners. But it should be noted that one of the objectives of Kagisano is to expand agricultural production, particularly with a view to increasing cash incomes in the rural areas. Many people in rural Botswana depend on rearing cattle for their livelihood. Therefore, is it likely that the policy makers who are mostly foreign would understand the problems and fears of this rural population? Is the president serious when he talks of improving living conditions in the rural areas?

On the whole the overall employment picture in the country does not seem to reflect the hope and the optimism of the ideology of Kagisano. As we have already indicated, of the total labor force of over 250,000 in 1964 only 30,151 received cash wages. In 1968, out of a total population of 611,000 only 28,148 were wage earning, that is, 8.6 percent of the total population of working age. These figures are not very impressive if compared to neighboring Swaziland with 48,300 persons in wage employment in 1966 out of a total population of 374,600.[15]

TABLE 4.4

Manpower Demand and Supply in Botswana, 1972

Ministry/Department	Established Posts	Superscale: Local	Superscale: Expatriate	Superscale: Vacancy
Finance and Development Planning	13	2	10	1
Tsetse, Animal Health and Production, Land Utilization	9	—	9	—
Commerce, Industry and Water Affairs	4	2	2	—
Wildlife, Geological Surveys, Water Affairs	12	—	4	8
Buildings, Roads, etc.	11	—	8	3
Works and Communications	7	3	4	—
			Administrative	
State President	28	11	11	6
Finance and Development Planning	12	7	4	1
			Professional	
Finance and Development Planning	15	4	11	—
Medical	27	3	14	10
Tsetse, Animal Health and Production, Land Utilization	25	—	14	11
Education	24	4	12	8
Buildings, Roads, etc.	12	1	5	6

Source: Botswana, Ministry of Finance and Development Planning, *Manpower and Employment in Botswana* (Gaborone: Government Printer, 1973), pp. 112-13.

By 1971 the ratio of wage earners to population was 8.9 percent, which compares favorably with those for other African countries when 1968 figures are used; for example, Zambia 9 percent, Kenya 6 percent, Uganda 3.5 percent, and Tanzania 2.8 percent.[16] In 1972 the total number of permanent wage employees stood at just over 48,000 out of an increased population of over 600,000.[17] It has been estimated that in 1971 about the same number of people in the economically active group of the population who had wage employment (that is, about 48,000) migrated to South Africa, Rhodesia, Zambia, and other neighboring countries in search of work. Without this outflow of migrants it is assumed that the ranks of those in the traditional sector (that is, those who are not wage earners) would have been increased by 8 percent over the 1971 level. This shows the tremendous influence migration out of Botswana into neighboring countries has on the overall economy of the country, and on the size of the domestic labor force.[18] Although it may be politically undesirable, the government has made no attempts to reduce the rate of migration—maybe in order to achieve social harmony, which is the prime tenet of the national ideology.

However, the picture does not look totally grim, for the implementation of the ideology of Kagisano has some positive results. We have already noted that prior to 1961 there was no policy of localization of the labor force and even junior-level posts such as typists, electricians, and registration clerks were filled by expatriates, mainly British and white South Africans. Ten years of political independence is understandably too short to completely change the skilled manpower problems in Botswana, or in any developing country in Africa. President Khama was therefore realistic enough to say in 1964, while commenting on the question of localization of the labor force: "We shall, of course, continue to have expatriates for quite some time and it would be an irresponsible assumption to think that even when we attain self-government next year, every person who is an expatriate will no longer be required."[19] He accordingly set 1990 as the target date for self-sufficiency in high-level manpower.

In spite of the present dominance of high-level professions by expatriates, notable progress has been made in the lower technical professions and sectors, as we have already indicated by the increase in trade and homecraft schools from 2 in 1965 to 41 in 1973.

Also, although the agricultural policy makers are foreign, since independence Botswana has paid particular attention to the training of technicians in agriculture (commercial farming), on which the economy of the country almost entirely depends. In 1967 it established the Botswana Agricultural College and in 1970 the Cooperative Development Center. In addition, youth brigades and community development departments assisted in vocational training. Prior to 1968 private organizations had obtained skilled labor from outside the country. But since the launching of the 1968-73 National Development Plan, the government has insisted on in-service or on-the-job training for local people and private firms are expected to sponsor trainees at the

Botswana Training Center in Gaborone. Although it will take more effort, money, and time to educate the 60,000 to 70,000 farmers in the country, the present situation is far from that of the colonial administration when agriculture was never mentioned in the primary and secondary educational systems. With this new emphasis on agriculture, the government objective of improving agriculture eventually may be achieved.

We have also indicated earlier the economic dependence of Botswana on South Africa and the tact and tolerance—call it "realism" if you will—with which President Khama has trotted along, even unwillingly, with his big neighbor. Not only do Botswana's migrant workers feed the farms and industries of South Africa, but both countries, at least as of 1970, still have a customs union, a currency union, and more important, a common market for technical skills. The dependence of Botswana's economy on that of South Africa, especially in the provision of high-skill manpower in the former's cattle industry will persist for some time to come. This is not to say, of course, that President Khama is not seeking to minimize this dependence. While Botswana sets 1990 as a target date for self-sufficiency in high-level manpower, it expects to completely localize the public sector long before then. To do this will require tact and understanding on the part of the expatriates. Here the ideology of Kagisano, which calls for social harmony, becomes functional.

Economic Development

One question becomes appropriate at this stage. Have the Batswana benefited from Botswana's development? In other words, does the ideology of Kagisano mean anything to the Batswana? As already indicated, the British throughout their protectorateship of Botswana never considered it worth educating the African population or instituting any kind of serious development in the country. Therefore it should not be surprising that at independence every strategic sector of the economy was in the control of expatriates, notably, white South Africans and British. The Batswana were inevitably relegated to the lower-paying jobs.

As in the case of most other African countries upon obtaining independence, Botswana's development aim was spelled out in the National Development Plan to

1. achieve an average annual increase of 6 percent in national income (3 percent per capita);
2. free the country of the need for grant-in-aid of current budgetary expenditure in the shortest time possible (no more than 15 years); and

3. as a long-term objective, to achieve a more equitable income among the people.[20]

These aims are in line with the ideology of Kagisano.

After ten years of independence how has the country fared in the achievement of the first objective? In the 1965/66 financial year, which coincided with independence, the GDP at current market prices was R37.85 million;* in 1967/68 it was R42.1 million. In 1969 the GDP at constant 1970 market prices was $75.5 million; rose to $83.0 million in 1970; and by 1971 it stood at $97.7 million. Thus the annual growth rate in the 1969/70 financial year was 5.7 percent and in the 1970/71 period it jumped to 17.7 percent, well above 6 percent planned in the 1968-73 National Development Plan. In 1971/72 the GDP was R 100.4 million.[21]

The buoyancy of the economy within this period has inevitably affected per capita incomes. In 1966 per capita income in Botswana was $86.00; in 1969 it had risen to $124.60 at 1970 constant market prices; it again rose slightly to $127.70 in 1970; and by the end of 1970 it stood at $145.80. Since 1969, when the objectives of the 1968-73 Development Plan in respect to national income and per capita earnings were to be pursued, this means an annual growth rate in per capita GDP of 2.5 percent in 1969-70 and 14.2 percent in 1970-71. In 1972 this rose again by 14.9 percent thus making Botswana one of only 9 out of 41 African countries that achieved the target set for the Second Development Decade with respect to the growth of GDP at constant factor cost.[22]

With regard to the second objective of the 1968-73 plan, let us first note that right from the days of its protectorateship Botswana depended on grants from the Imperial government to operate even the barest services. After 1956 it depended on grants-in-aid to balance its annual budget. In the 1955/57 budgetary year the amount of subsidy was £140,000. By 1965/66 the amount rose sharply to almost £2 million.[23]

Because of the natural poverty in mineral resources, the dearth of skilled manpower, the general high degree of illiteracy, coupled with the smallness of its population and the persistent dependence on grants-in-aid to have even the barest services function, it was generally wondered whether Botswana could survive on its own, whether independence was worthwhile and not an unnecessary painful luxury. Nevertheless, President Khama himself was optimistic about his country's future. On the question of external aid he said that "we have accepted with gratitude the assistance of the many friendly countries which have provided us with aid. But it has been aid provided for development programmes which we have been able to plan in accordance with our own values and our own priorities."[24]

*1 U.S. dollar = .87R

The following figures show Botswana's dependence on external aid and investment. In the 1966/67 financial year U. K. grants had risen to the peak amount of R 4, 279, 140; in 1967/68 the amount declined precipitously to R 2, 898, 069; and in the 1968/69 year in which President Khama spelled out his government's objective to free the country of grants-in-aid, the amount had further declined to R 2, 574, 013. [25] But in 1969/70 the amount rocketed to R 9, 024, 000. The government aggressively solicited aid to implement the Development Plan despite the President's stated objective to rely less on foreign aid. But in 1970/71 the figure again fell to a mere R 498, 000 before climbing back to a modest R1, 918, 000.

Perhaps we also can have an idea of Botswana's progress in freeing herself of grants-in-aid by examining the strength of her domestic funds over the years immediately before and after independence.

In 1944/45 recurrent revenue from domestic sources was R 769, 000; it rose to R 1, 935, 000 in 1957/58; and by 1969/70 the amount had climbed to R 7, 032, 000. In 1969/70 the figure was R 10, 797, 000; in 1970/71, R 11, 709, 000; in 1971/72, R 17, 406, 000. In 1969/70 the total revenue (that is grants-in-aid and loans) was R 22, 517, 000; in 1970/71 it fell to R 13, 512, 000; and in 1971/72 it went up a bit to R 19, 895, 000. The fall was because of a cutback in grants-in-aid and loans. [26] Although Botswana still relies on aid, it is making every effort to be self-reliant. Whether it eventually would be independent of external aid is yet to be seen.

In respect to the third objective of the Development Plan aim, Table 4. 5 on wage differentials among different sectors shows how income is distributed in the country. We have already indicated that the per capita income in 1966 was $86. 00 and by 1971 it had risen to $145. 80.

TABLE 4. 5

African-Expatriate Wage Differentials, 1973
(per month in Rands)

Sector	Citizens	Expatriates*
Agriculture	25	175
Mining and Quarrying	52	513
Manufacturing	42	437
Construction	55	508
Finance	65	444
Education	50	113
Total	289	2, 190

*"Expatriates" also include a number of black Africans.
Source: Botswana, Ministry of Finance and Development Planning, Manpower and Employment in Botswana (Gaborone: Government Printer, 1973), p. 54.

Table 4.5 shows that the citizens earn less than the expatriates in all sectors of the economy. It also reveals two other aspects of the problem of income distribution. First is the inequality between sectors, for example, between agriculture and mining or construction or between manufacturing and finance; and second is the inequality of education for Africans and expatriates alike. The differentials between agriculture and, say, finance or manufacturing imply the differentials between rural and urban. The rural areas still do not have a fair share of the proceeds of development, despite the government promise to improve the rural living standards. Perhaps not implied in Table 4.5 are the differentials between levels of education. Table 4.6 therefore portrays these differentials.

TABLE 4.6

Wage Differentials in Levels of Education in Private and Parastatal Sectors in Botswana, 1973 (mean monthly earnings in Rands)

Levels of Actual Education and Training	Batswana	Non-Batswana
Degree plus training	228	303
Degree	226	292
Form V plus training	156	316
Form III	70	253
Form I	44	305
Up to standard 7	46	182
All unskilled workers	60	266
Other workers (excluding domestics)	28	—
Domestics	15	—

Source: Botswana, Ministry of Finance and Development Planning, Manpower and Employment in Botswana (Gaborone: Government Printer, 1973), p. 54-56.

The wage differentials in the public sector are only slightly equitable. The highest-paid Batswana earns about 20 times as much as the least paid. Comparative figures for the developed countries reveal the highest levels are not that much greater than the lowest levels. For example, the ratio between the earnings of a laborer and a top civil servant is about 1:12 in Britain and about 1:15 in the United States.[27]

The discrepancies between the Batswana and non-Batswana unskilled as well as Forms I through V are also revealing. We have earlier stated the high rate of migration of Batswana (mainly the semi-skilled and unskilled) to neighboring countries, especially South Africa, in search of employment. Nevertheless, the government has to pay high wages to attract similar but expatriate labor. Would this government practice bring about social harmony which is implicit in the national ideology? Whatever the case is, the above statistics show the levels of inequality that still exist in a country of just slightly more than a million. Whether the situation would change, according to the president, is no matter of urgency. (We have already quoted his comments on the distribution of wealth.)[28]

Social Development

It is not surprising, then, that in spite of the tremendous efforts to hold her own, registering moderately impressive GDP and per capita income increases, Botswana is still one of the least developed countries in Africa. On the eve of independence, admittedly a disastrous year for agriculture because of droughts, 300,000 Batswana were on World Food Program relief.[29] (The entire population at that date was 543,000.) In spite of the government's apparent attention to agriculture, in 1968 large numbers of Batswana were (and still are) not self-sufficient in food supplies, such as maize and sorghum.[30]

Also the literacy/illiteracy rate is still not impressive. The 1968-73 National Development Plan, using the 1964 census figures, states that approximately 75 percent of the population was illiterate. This would seem a much higher record at that date than that for most African countries, although we should not take the figures too seriously since the very small population of the country would naturally boost its overall literacy rate. By 1969 the illiteracy rate had declined only to 72 percent, in spite of the government's declared policy to expand the educational system.

On the basis of development objectives as expressed in the 1968-73 National Development Plan, the improvement of social services, though not ignored, does not seem to command any priority attention. As recently as 1974 there were only 12 hospitals, 1 mental home, 14 health centers, 33 clinics, 3 dispensaries, and 141 health posts. The number of inhabitants per doctor as of 1969 was estimated to be 35,000.[31]

With regard to the consumption of durable goods there has been a steady but slight increase since independence. Table 4.7 on the possession of vehicles gives an indication of this rate of increase. Even the government expenditure on vehicles has increased over the years, even though it incurred no expenditure on vehicles before and immediately after independence (1966). There are no available statistics for 1968 because that was the year that the 1968-73 National Development Plan was launched. There has also been an increase in the use of the telephone. For example, in 1970 there were 3, 680 telephones and by 1974 the number had jumped to 6, 699. What the statistics fail to show is whether these telephones were owned by expatriates or Batswana. By the sheer rule of thumb it is likely that telephone owners are those who earn high incomes, and these, according to the above statistics, are mostly foreigners. As a result, the Batswana themselves are not the real beneficiaries of these social amenities.

TABLE 4.7

Possession of Vehicles in Botswana, 1965-73

Year	Number of Private Vehicles	Number of Government Vehicles
1965	3, 884	—
1966	4, 302	—
1967	4, 992	1, 493
1969	5, 681	1, 273
1971	6, 462	—
1973	8, 357	1, 610

Source: Botswana, *Statistical Abstract, 1974* (Gaborone: Government Printer, 1974), p. 78.

It may be appropriate at this stage to ask who controls the economy of Botswana. From our discussion so far this question seems either irrelevant or superfluous. Before independence in 1966 there were almost no industries. The import and export trade was in the hands of expatriates, mainly South Africans. The extent of this control is shown in a 1955 survey that reveals that 74 percent of the general dealers' licences were held by foreigners (chief among them South Africans and Britons), 15 percent by Africans, and 11 percent by Asians. Thus most of the badly needed capital was sent out of the country in the form of interests, profits, and dividends to headquarters in South Africa or Britain.[32] The only way Botswana has tried to make up for this outflow of funds has been through the renegotiation of the customs union for more equitable terms.

CONCLUSION

As a result of geographical, historical, political, and economic ties with South Africa and the advantages that accrue from those ties and the absence, or difficulty, of cultivating an alternative viable market at the present time, Botswana seems a long way from developing a truly independent economy. Not only does a large segment of Botswana's labor (the migrants) depend on South African industries for their livelihood; not only do a large number of Batswana still depend on South African educational facilities and technicians for their vital cattle industry, the two countries belong to the same monetary and customs unions. So far, Botswana seems to enjoy the advantages and no wonder its government considers it irresponsible to think of breaking such ties now for political reasons. It seems all President Khama wants to do, can do, at the present is to minimize the dependence. But as long as the dependence continues, Kagisano is the most practical ideology for Botswana. Whether the Batswana would like to play a marginal role, which this ideology seems to have conferred on them, is anybody's guess.

NOTES

1. E. S. Mungner, Bechuanaland: Pan-African Outpost or Bantu Homeland? (London: Institute for Race Relations, 1965), p. 18.
2. Ibid., p. 19.
3. Botswana, Ministry of Finance and Development Planning, National Development Plan, 1973-78, Part I (Gaborone: Government Printer, 1973), p. 37.
4. Martin Minogue and Judith Molloy, eds., African Aims and Attitudes: Selected Documents (Cambridge: Cambridge University Press, 1974), pp. 166-67.
5. Botswana, Ministry of Finance and Development Planning, op. cit., p. 37.
6. Ibid.
7. Ibid., pp. 40-41.
8. United Nations, Statistical and Economic Bulletin for Africa, no. 6 (1971), p. 86.
9. Botswana, National Development Plan 1968-73 (Gaborone: Government Printer, 1968), p. 53.
10. Richard P. Stevens, Lesotho, Botswana and Swaziland: The Former High Commission Territories in Southern Africa (London: Pall Mall Press, 1967), p. 161.
11. R. E. Culbertson, Senior Seminar in Foreign Policy: Bechuanaland — Resources for Nationhood and Development, mimeographed (Washington, D. C.: Foreign Service Institute, 1966), pp. 20-22.
12. Botswana, Statistical Abstract, 1974 (Gaborone: Government Printer, 1974), pp. 20-22.
13. Culbertson, op. cit., p. 24.
14. Ibid., pp. 22-25.

15. P. Smit, Resources and Development (Pretoria: African Institute of South Africa, 1970), pp. 65-66.

16. Botswana, Ministry of Finance and Development Planning, Manpower and Employment in Botswana (Gaborone: Government Printer, 1973), p. 4.

17. Ibid., p. 15.

18. Ibid., pp. 7-9.

19. Bechuanaland, Report on Localisation and Training (Gaborone: Government Printer, 1966).

20. Botswana, National Development Plan, 1968-73, op. cit.

21. See United Nations, Survey of Economic Conditions in Africa (New York: UN, 1972), p. 45; and Botswana, Statistical Abstract, 1974 (Gaborone: Government Printer, 1974), p. 106.

22. UN, Survey of Economic Conditions in Africa, op. cit., p. 54.

23. Culbertson, op. cit., p. 14.

24. Minogue and Molloy, op. cit., p. 165.

25. Smit, op. cit., p. 144.

26. Botswana, Statistical Abstract, 1972 (Gaborone, Government Printer, 1972), table 42.

27. Ukandi G. Damachi, Nigerian Modernization: The Colonial Legacy (New York: The Third Press, 1972), p. 105.

28. Smit, op. cit.

29. Culbertson, op. cit., p. 16.

30. Smit, op. cit., p. 195.

31. United Nations, Economic Bulletin for Africa (New York: UN, January 1964), p. 89.

32. Smit, op. cit., pp. 168-69.

CHAPTER

5

JULIUS NYERERE: UJAMAA—SOCIALISM AND RURAL DEVELOPMENT IN TANZANIA

Tanganyika (that is, mainland Tanzania) became independent and a sovereign member of the Commonwealth on December 9, 1961. In 1962, it became a Republic. Zanzibar obtained independence on December 9, 1963, and on April 27, 1964 Tanganyika and Zanzibar formed the United Republic of Tanganyika and Zanzibar. On October 29 of the same year the union was christened Tanzania, with Nyerere as president. After this brief historical review we may now proceed with presenting Nyerere's development ideology.

UJAMAA

"Ujamaa" is literally translated as "familyhood" or "brotherhood." In Ujamaa Nyerere is concerned with socialism and traditional African society and problems of stratification in society. The essential goal of Ujamaa is to build a society in which all members have equal rights and equal opportunities and where social justice is practiced. To create this kind of society Nyerere believes that it has to be built on the firm foundation of the three principles of the Ujamaa family: respect, community life, and an obligation to work. In addition to these principles there is need to develop the knowledge and instruments necessary to overcome the poverty that was prevalent in traditional African society. In other words, there is an urgent need to modernize the means of production in order to guarantee increased output per worker.[1] It is important, he reiterates, for the attitudes of traditional African socialism to be regained, modified, and applied to the new societies being built.[2]

Nyerere recognizes that the adoption of such a plan will not bring about immediate development and/or industrialization. He still realizes that for the foreseeable future the vast majority of Tanzanians will continue to live and find their wherewithal in the rural areas. The land therefore is the only basis of Tanzania's development. Accordingly, Tanzanian socialism must be firmly based on the land in order to ensure its success.

If this type of socialism is to succeed, the Tanzanians have to fulfill certain essential conditions. The first of these is hard work, which, according to Nyerere, has no substitute especially as Tanzania is basically a poor country lacking large accumulations of capital that can be invested in agricultural labor-saving devices or in increased productivity. It is then obligatory on Tanzanians to rely "on their hands and brains"[3] to develop.

In addition, there must be an efficient and democratic system of local government so that the people make their own decisions on the things that affect them directly. This would enable them to establish control over community decisions and ensure their responsibility for carrying them out. Yet this local control has to be organized in such a way that the nation is united and working together for common needs and for the maximum development of the whole society.

Consequently, for Nyerere, it is vital that the principles upon which the traditional extended family was based be reactivated. For a start, extended family villages are to be established and with time they will be developed into larger communities than was traditionally the case. Also, modern knowledge must be applied by these communities, and ways and means have to be found to break the barriers that previously existed between different groups so that they cooperate on the achievement of the major tasks of development. The basis of rural life in Tanzania has to be "the practice of cooperation in its widest sense in living, in working, and in distribution. . . ."[4]

To ensure such a cooperation by different people, Ujamaa farms and communities are to form the basis for the rural economy and to set the social pattern for the country as a whole. This means that most farming needs are to be done by groups of people who live and work as a community. This community is the traditional family group or any other group of people living according to these Ujamaa principles articulated by Nyerere:

> The land this community farmed would be called "our land" by all the members; the crops they produced on that land would be "our crops"; it would be "our shop" which provided individual members with the day-to-day necessities from outside; "our workshop" which made the bricks from which houses and other buildings were constructed. . . .[5]

Nyerere hopes that such living and working in communities could transform the living standards of Tanzanians. Although optimistic about the outcome of this system, he cautions that Tanzania would not automatically become wealthy; there is hope, however, that her citizens could all become a little richer than before independence. But most important, any increase in the amount of wealth produced under this system would not only belong to the Tanzanians but would also strengthen their traditional equality and security.

Ujamaa socialism with its emphasis on village communities therefore would be in full practice in Tanzania. The essential element in these communities would be the equality of all members, and the members' self-government in all matters that concern their own affairs. Such a system would ensure that Tanzania is a socialist nation.

Socialism, like democracy, is construed by Nyerere to be an attitude of mind. It is this attitude of mind, rather than a rigid adherence to a standard political pattern, that is needed to ensure that people care for each other's welfare. African socialism, to Nyerere, is distinguished from capitalism, which seeks to build a happy society on the basis of exploitation of man by man; and it is equally opposed to doctrinaire socialism, which seeks to build a happy society on a philosophy of inevitable conflict between man and man. The foundation of African socialism is the extended family, which regards all men as brethren—as members of an ever-extending family.

On the whole Nyerere hopes that the implementation of his Ujamaa ideology would transform Tanzania from a nation of individual peasant producers who are gradually adopting the incentives and the ethics of the capitalist system to a nation of Ujamaa villages where the people cooperate directly in small groups and where these small groups cooperate together for joint enterprises.[6] How does he hope to achieve this?

PROGRAMS OF ACTION

Nyerere himself realizes that the farmers in Tanzania, like those elsewhere in the world, have learned to be cautious about new ideas however attractive they may sound. Hence he points out that it is only through experience that novel ideas become acceptable. Consequently, he emphasizes certain caveats that would help in the implementation of his Ujamaa ideology. The first of these is that socialist communities cannot be established by compulsion but by persuasion. Farmers are to be persuaded to grow a certain acreage of a particular crop until they realize that this brings them a more secure living. Indeed, viable socialist communities can only be established with willing members. The task of leadership and of government is to encourage the farmers and promote this kind of development.

The second caveat is that mere persuasive words may not be enough to convince established farmers to adopt the Ujamaa village system. The farmers need to see for themselves the advantages of working and living together before they trust their future to this organization of life. In particular, before giving up their individual plots of land they will wish to see that the system of working together really benefits everyone. It becomes important for groups of young men to experiment on the new system of Ujamaa villages.

With these two caveats, Nyerere and his party, Tanganyika African National Union (TANU), set up the national objectives to guide their development efforts. The amended version of the TANU Constitution of 1961 listed the basic objectives as "the elimination of poverty, disease, and ignorance, and the insurance of a decent standard of living for all citizens."[7]

To implement these objectives the following programs of action have been drawn up. First, Ujamaa villages (privately owned plantations by groups of citizens) and kulaks (state farms) have been established.

Second, the peasants and the workers through their cooperatives and government are to control the major means of production. It is therefore necessary to ensure that the ruling party is a party of peasants and workers. Some of these major means of production are the land, forests, mineral resources, art, electricity, and so on.[8]

Third, good leadership is inevitable if the ideals of Ujamaa and the development objectives are to be attained. The party headquarters is charged with training leaders from the national level down to the leaders of the Ujamaa villages so that all may understand the political and economic policies. Leaders must show good examples to the rest of the people through their actions and in their own lives. To ensure this a leadership code has been instituted stipulating that every TANU and government leader must be either a peasant or a worker and should in no way be associated with the practices of capitalism or feudalism. Leaders are also prohibited from holding shares or directorships in any company. They are not to receive two or more salaries or own rentable apartment houses. Finally, the term "leader" in this context comprises the following: "Members of the TANU National Executive Committee; Ministers, Members of Parliament, Senior Officials of Organizations affiliated to TANU, Senior Officials of Para-Statal Organizations, all those appointed or elected under any clause of the TANU Constitution, Councillors, and Civil Servants in high and middle cadres."[9] (In short, to Nyerere, "leader" means man, or a man and his wife, a woman, or a woman and her husband.)

Fourth is the provision of an educational system that is much more Tanzanian in content, that is, which fosters the social goals of living together, and working together, for the common good. It is aimed at preparing the young people to play a dynamic and constructive role in the development of a society in which all members share fairly in the good and bad fortune of the group, and in which progress is measured in terms of human well-being, not prestige buildings, cars, or other such things, whether publicly or privately owned. Tanzanian education seeks to inculcate a sense of commitment to the total community and to help the pupils accept the values appropriate to Tanzania's future.

Finally, in order to ensure the implementation of the policies of socialism and self-reliance, the planning and control of development are decentralized. The regions and districts are to plan and implement local development activities as well as administer local affairs with a minimum of interference from Dar es Salaam, and "new development councils and committees" have been set up to increase the people's participation in decision making. This decentralized system hopefully will increase the reality of democracy and thus bring power closer to the people, thereby making the institutions of development more efficient. We may now ask how the country has performed since independence with such well-articulated programs of action.

EVALUATION: PERFORMANCE OF DEVELOPMENT IDEOLOGY

Labor Force

An examination of Tanzanian labor force statistics not only will help us understand the rationale of Nyerere's ideology but also will give us an insight into Tanzania's development trend since independence in 1961. The population census of 1957 showed 56 percent of African males and 59 percent of African females to be over 14—about 5 million out of an estimated population of 9 million. By 1961, the last year before independence, fewer than 400, 000 of these were working as wage or salary earners in the modern sector, and of these only about 20, 000 were employed in factories. About half of the wage and salary earners were engaged as agricultural workers on plantations or estates.

Thus, by the time the British handed over power, more than 90 percent of the population were rural dwellers making their living as subsistence farmers. The picture had not changed much by 1965, a year after the union between Tanganyika and Zanzibar. The population had risen to 11. 37 million with an urban population of 4. 8 percent and rural 95. 2 percent. This picture persisted even up to 1972 when the population had increased to 14 million; the rural population was still over 90 percent while the urban was 5. 7 percent.[10] Between 1960 and 1970 the average annual growth rate of the urban population was 5. 8 percent while the percentage of the economically active population employed in the agricultural sector was 90. 8 percent—a good reason for Nyerere's ideology of "socialism and rural development."

A further breakdown of the labor force participation rates since the union would tend to justify Nyerere's emphasis on rural development. In 1965, of the 5. 5 million people of working age, only 333, 755 (6. 1 percent) were in paid employment. In 1966 this stood at about 335, 000, and by 1971 it had risen to 402, 000. This means wage employment has grown over the period by an annual average rate of 4 percent, even though the population grew at an annual rate of 2.8 percent over the same period.[11] One may wonder why the labor force statistics of Tanzania are so much different from her neighbors such as Kenya and Zambia.

Whereas Zambia is rich in natural resources, especially copper, Tanzania is relatively poor and depends mainly on agriculture. However, although Tanzania has surplus land (compared with the size of her population) the fertile areas are found only along the mountain slopes of the Kilimanjaro-Usambara region, the central core of the country being mainly arid. This natural incidence constituted a grave problem of communication before independence. As it is to be expected, when the Europeans came into the country they settled in these cool, fertile highlands. And although these Europeans had intentions of settling there permanently, they made no attempts whatsoever to tackle the immense communications problems that beset the country by linking up the highlands with the rest of the country. Also because of the European intent that persisted even into the 1950s, there was no urgent desire to educate the Africans to prepare them for the leadership role. The cumulative result was that Tanzania had two serious problems of development to deal with: (1) the natural poverty of the land, that is, the lack of any significant mineral resources, and (2) lack of skilled manpower to deal with the problems caused by the natural incidence of poverty. It is reasonable, then, that any evaluation of the development process in Tanzania be undertaken with these two conditions in mind.

The first condition—with the realization that the country could not adequately attract foreign investment and therefore there was a special need to carefully, prudently, and rationally utilize its scarce resources—weighed heavily on the minds of the Tanzanian leadership in deciding on the African socialist path for which the country has come to be known today. Notwithstanding, Tanzania has had a lot of manpower problems different in scope and circumstances from those faced in Zambia.

It has been indicated that because of the European settlers' intention to settle permanently in Tanganyika, and because the Africans themselves, even well into the 1950s before Nyerere's TANU became more active, had expected to remain colonialized for a few more decades, the country was unprepared in terms of skilled manpower when independence was deemed possible and when it was obtained finally.

Moreover, the problems of indigenous skilled manpower, although perhaps much better than in the case of Zambia, at least as far as their numbers went, were more complex and sensitive because they derived coloration from the complexity of the society itself. Although the African population was overwhelming--98 to 99 percent--the other 1 or 2 percent,[12] which comprised mainly Asians and Europeans, dominated the modern and public sector and the educational institutions.

It may be pointed out here that perhaps what happened to the African population was as much caused by colonial historical forces as self-induced—self-induced in the sense that at a time the Asians were pressing the colonial government to subsidize their educational efforts, most Africans were rejecting education as an attempt to sabotage their traditional values.

Education

Current figures on Tanzanian education and manpower are not available, but the following, though old, are revealing. On the eve of independence in 1961 the levels of secondary education shown in Table 5.1 has been attained.

TABLE 5.1

Levels of Secondary Education Attained in Tanzania, 1961

Secondary School Enrolment, 1961	African	Asian	European
Form 1 entry	2,163	1,914	119
Form 4	687	700	60

Source: Guy Hunter, Education for a Developing Region: A Study in East Africa (London: Allen and Unwin, 1963).

By the same year the number of secondary schools by race was as follows: 42 African, 13 European, 36 Asian, and 3 other non-native. There were therefore more secondary school for foreigners than for Africans.

With such structural educational problems, it is not surprising that Tanzania is one of the very few, if there are any other, African countries to truly overhaul its educational system after independence. Immediately after independence school systems on racial structures were abolished -- all being unified into a single system. After the Arusha Declaration,* Tanzania took a lead in structuring its educational system to its overall development ideology.

* The Arusha Declaration, a document setting out Tanzania's broad policy on socialist development, was drafted by Nyerere in 1967 and adopted by TANU in the same year.

In 1966 and 1969 the total enrolment for Africans, Asians, Europeans, and others stood at 6, 377 and 7, 149 in Form I and 4, 723 and 6, 328 in Form IV respectively.[13] In 1966/67, the enrolment of Tanzanian students at the universities of East Africa for degree courses was 791, while in 1969/70 it had risen to 1, 769. The enrolment in foreign universities and institutions was 1, 128; in 1969/70 it stood at 604.[14] The number had decreased because of Tanzania's policy for educating for self-reliance. The implication of this policy is that the "education provided by Tanzania for the students of Tanzania must serve the purposes of Tanzania."[15]

It will be noticed that after independence in 1961, especially after the formation of the Tanzanian Union in 1964, the government had made great efforts to speed the education of its population. Nonetheless, Tanzania is still far from solving its educational and manpower problems; for example, in spite of the said acceleration in educating the African population, as late as 1969 the staffing of post-primary schools was still in the hands of non-Africans. In 1966 there were 368 citizens and 919 noncitizens on the secondary school staffs. By 1969 the ratio was still in favor of the noncitizen staff, 851 citizens to 1, 096 noncitizens. This imbalance also existed in the teacher training colleges. In 1966 there were 101 citizen staff members and 106 noncitizen, but by 1969 the number of the citizen staff members had increased to 153 while that of the noncitizen had decreased to 75.[16]

While discussing Zambia (Chapter 2) we indicated the high rate of illiteracy in Tanzania in comparison, noting that in 1961 only 10 percent of primary school-age population was enroled in school. Thus in 1962 there was about 86 percent illiteracy among the men and 95 percent among the women. In 1961 in Tanganyika, a country with a population of about 9 million, only an estimated 407 African boys and 32 girls, 400 Asian boys and 160 girls received school certificate passes. In 1962 only 106 received Higher School Certificates (HSC). It should be pointed out that there were only four schools in the whole of Tanganyika that were offering HSC. However, in 1964 the country had 464 HSC candidates, among whom 370 gained university admission.

Even by 1970 the illiterate population, which was 86 percent of the men and 95 percent of the women in 1962, had declined to only 85 percent cumulatively, in spite of the fact that since independence, and especially after the Arusha Declaration, great emphasis has been placed on primary, adult, and rural education. In 1964 the chances of a child going to school were 46 percent but by 1969 this had risen only to 47 percent, partly because of high population growth.[17]

These statistics portray the very serious skilled manpower shortage that existed in Tanzania, especially among the African population before and immediately after independence. Table 5. 2 shows the 1964 occupational structure of Category "A" Manpower, that is, the category for which entry requirement normally would be a university degree.

TABLE 5. 2

Occupational Structure in Tanzania,
"Category A" Manpower, 1964

Type	African	European	Asian	Vacancy
Science	153	1,114	265	302
Arts	324	818	243	117
Total	477 (14)*	1,932 (58)	508 (15)	419 (13)

*Numbers in parentheses indicate percentage of total.

Source: Robert L. Thomas, Survey of the High-Level Manpower Requirements and Resources for 5-Year Development Plan 1964-65 to 1968-69 (Tanzanian government publication).

As shown by the table's figures, the skilled labor force, including the upper levels of government and business, was in control of Europeans and Asians: The Asians filled most of the intermediate posts in the government and controlled much of the commercial and industrial sectors. The skilled manpower was therefore exceedingly foreign at independence and shortly afterward.

"Localization"

The policy of Africanization that had been instituted shortly after independence was meant to correct the racial imbalance of the skilled work force. The question has been whether, with the skilled labor force so much in the hands of non-Africans, Tanzania would carry out a swift and radical Africanization policy. This realization may have influenced President Nyerere's thinking when in January 1964 he announced the change from "Africanization" to "localization," an attempt to stave off a sudden exodus of Europeans and Asians who constituted the highly needed high-level manpower.

So the Tanzanian answer to "localization" was to group people together in Ujamaa villages, where "they would live together; they would farm together; market together; and undertake the provision of local services and small local services and small local requirements as a community."[18] By 1972 there were about 400 Ujamaa villages, in which lived 11 percent of the population of the Tanzanian mainland, and the movement was being promoted region by region. In July 1972

"Operation Kigoma" was to begin, in terms of which 8,000 families were to be settled in 23 Ujamaa villages. Ten dispensaries and some primary schools were to be provided and 24,000 acres to be plowed. Phase Two of "Operation Dodoma" would involve the settlement of an additional 56,000 families.[19]

Opinion is divided among development experts on the success of the Ujamaa villages. For example, Guy Routh's conclusion is one of tempered optimism. He states that "as one might expect, reports from the villages tell widely divergent stories. Some have been highly successful, with outstanding and dedicated men using their gifts to inspire their fellows, but sometimes the spirit of Ujamaa has been doused by the over-enthusiasm of a Regional Commissioner."[20]

Henry Bienen also shares in this conclusion, for he writes that "it is of great importance that the ideals Nyerere expressed in 'Ujamaa' have not taken hold. 'Ujamaa' has remained a statement of ideals; it has not been taken as a call to action."[21]

Fred Burke, on the other hand, expresses a more positive optimism about the success of Ujamaa. According to him, Ujamaa has a comprehensible, flexible, and dignified ethnic for programs and policies that spring from complex physical and psychological needs of an emerging and dynamic people.[22] Whatever the case is, Ujamaa presents a statement of human values that is impressive enough to justify not only the Tanzanian but also many other different government policies. It addresses itself to the hydra-headed social ills of Tanzania and tends to provide a program for solving them. Whether these social ills are being solved as fast as the Tanzanians may wish is another question.

Nevertheless, the style and content of the Ujamaa ideology have also proved important, and despite the low literacy rates, for one thing, contact between the center and the districts has increased (thanks to decentralization). Many people are being brought into contact with the center for the first time, but the center is still very limited in the services it can provide and the tangible results it can bring to the people. Its relationships with the masses and the interrelationships--vertically between TANU people at local, district, regional, and central levels, and horizontally from place to place--are in the realm of discussing problems and thinking about what can be done and the way to do it. The way in which problems are presented is thus important if the pace of social development is to be accelerated.

Income

Has Nyerere's ideology of African socialism somehow been able to bring development to the average Tanzanian? We have indicated that at the time of independence Tanzania had a very high illiteracy rate. However, although current data are not available, it has been widely known that Tanzania has placed special emphasis on primary, secondary, and adult education. We have also pointed out that because of educational setbacks and the pattern of colonial administration the Africans had a very low participation rate in the modern sector of the economy. Not only that, they were mainly employed in the lower-paying jobs.

In 1961 African per capita income was estimated to be somewhere between $17.00 and $22.00. The African population, which was over 98 percent of the total, was responsible for 70 percent of the GDP. Thus 97 percent of the African wage earners made less than $100.00 a month.[23]

Since independence, however, and with the Africanization of the economy and the shift toward "socialism" the pattern of participation in the modern sector by Tanzanians and their pattern and levels of income have changed tremendously. Earnings in the wage/salary sector have risen quite fast since 1962. For example, employees earning less than 100 Tanzanian Shillings (T. Sh.) in 1962 per month declined from 169,000 in 1962 to only 15,000 in 1966, while those receiving from T. Sh. 150-199 per month increased from 32,300 in 1962 to 72,000 in 1966.[24] In percentage terms, those in the income group of under T. Sh. 150 (in both private and public sectors) had declined from 27 percent in 1968 to 18.6 percent in 1970; those in T. Sh. 150-199 declined from 28.9 percent in 1989 to 24.5 percent in 1970; but those in T. Sh. 200-399 increased from 28.1 percent in 1968 to 37.5 percent in 1970. The trend in wage-rate groups therefore shows a continuous shift from lower income groups to upper income groups because the Tanzanian development path is broadening and the fruits of development are fairly distributed in line with the national socialist philosophy.

TABLE 5.3

Average Monthly Earnings of Foreigners and Nationals in Tanzania, 1972
(in Tanzanian shillings)

Sector	Average Earning, Foreigners	Average Earning, Nationals	Foreign/ National
Enterprise	1,349	329	4.1
Public	1,232	352	3.5
Economy as a whole	1,320	340	3.9

Source: Teshome Mulat, "A Review of Income Distribution Questions in Six Eastern Africa Countries" in East African Regional Workshop on Social Aspects of Employment Promotion (Geneva: International Institute for Labour Studies, mimeographed, 1975), p. 20.

However, the distribution between foreigners and Tanzanian nationals is still skewed in favor of the foreigners. Table 5. 3 gives us the range of the skewness. The figures in the table demonstrate the level of inequality in the distribution in socialist Tanzania. This inequality is more pronounced at the level of the enterprise where the ratio between a foreigner's and national's wages is 4:1.

There are also wide differentials between rural-urban wages despite the thrust toward socialism and rural development. Table 5. 4 shows the levels of the differentials.

TABLE 5. 4

Rural-Urban Wage Differentials in Tanzania, 1972
(in Tanzanian shillings)

	Rural	Urban
Basic minimum wage	140	240
Annual consumption (expenditures per household)	1,700	6,108

Source: Teshome Mulat, "A Review of Income Distribution Questions in Six Eastern Africa Countries" in East African Regional Workshop on Social Aspects of Employment Promotion (Geneva: International Institute for Labour Studies, mimeographed, 1975), p. 12.

Here again the differentials between rural and urban wages are remarkable, almost 1 : 2 with regard to minimum wages. We should note that Tanzania's population is about 90 percent rural, depending heavily on agriculture. Such inequalities still exist in spite of serious government efforts to close the gap. For example, by as late as 1971 the top fifth wage/salary earners received 53. 6 percent and the bottom fifth 6. 6 percent of the total wage bill.[25]

Social Development

One is then tempted to ask, Is African socialism not working in Tanzania? Why is the government not achieving much success with its income distribution program? Nyerere has ideas and symbols through which others can understand the society in which they live and imagine the society of the future. While he has been the most ideological of the African leaders in that he has tried to formulate his ideas systematically and to provide symbolic frameworks, Nyerere is suspicious of creeds and dogmas and thus has been disinclined to create a blueprint for the new society. As a result, there are still traces of colonial habits with their emphasis on rigid stratification of society. Also, Nyerere has not very successfully married his ideas and symbols to programs of action. Several factors have contributed to this. For one thing, many of the programs of the TANU government are designed by expatriates who, while often sensitive to Nyerere's values, are largely unconcerned with providing a new symbolic framework. Economic constraints such as the lack of adequate capital for investment also operate in Tanzania to undermine many of Nyerere's ideas about social and economic equality. As he tries to take account of these constraints, he has made his formulations more pragmatic and less persuasive to those who must be his closest audience: the TANU middle-level leaders.[26] It is therefore not surprising that the programs of the TANU government as well as the definitions of TANU itself have been forged completely in the crucible of Nyerere's own ideals.

The divergence between the ideals of African socialism and the development and implementation of programs of action to attain these ideals extends to other factors in the social development profile. We have noted the inequality that exists in Tanzania in spite of the tremendous efforts to make life humane for all through socialism. We have also indicated the position of the Tanzanian worker before and immediately after independence and what it is now. Moreover, mention has been made of the level of literacy that existed than and what it is today. The health facilities in Tanzania have also been improving even though marginally since independence. Table 5.5 shows the improvements in public health facilities since 1961.

In 1969 the number of inhabitants per doctor was 20,000 (which is well above the one doctor for 10,000 considered appropriate by the World Health Organization). These figures are not very impressive when compared with Zambia's one doctor for 14,000, Uganda's one doctor for 7,800, or Kenya's one doctor for 9,500 inhabitants.[27]

It should be noted, however, that since 1972 Tanzania has stepped up the expansion of health facilities, especially in the rural areas, in accordance with the country's program of socialism. Tanzania certainly has a long way to go in providing adequate health care for every one of her citizens. Until recently there was no medical school in Tanzania to help accelerate the production of medical personnel. Thus progress in the health field seems to have been extremely slow. However, if we notice that the 1961-66 figures show a gradual decline in the number of medical personnel, occasioned perhaps by an emigration of European and Asian personnel, we are likely to temper our judgment and instead conclude with a note of optimism.

This optimism perhaps is justified with regard to the provision of housing for Tanzanians. It should be noted that every country in Africa, upon independence, has as one of its main objectives the provision of a decent quality of life, especially adequate housing, for every one of its citizens. Consequently, the government, in accordance with the socialist program, puts emphasis on self-help in developing the rural areas of the country and particularly in rural housing construction. Government assistance is only in the form of quality improvement.

TABLE 5.5

Public Health Facilities in Tanzania, 1961-72

	1961	1968	1969	1972
Medical practitioners (private and others)	590	657	—	916
Dentists	32	47	34	—
Pharmacists	50	46	54	—
Nurses and midwives	2,916	—	4,319	—
Number of hospitals (includes government, mission and industrial hospitals)	113	166	172	226
Dispensaries (includes government, mission, outpatient, etc. with less than or over 20 beds)	1,210	—	1,346	1,450
Clinics (antenatal and child health)	866	—	—	—
Number of beds	—	24,078	—	28,845

Source: Figures complied from Tanganyika Statistical Abstract 1962 (Dar es Salaam: Government Printer, 1963), pp. 153-55; Africa Annual Review, 1972 (London: African Journal Ltd.), pp. 127, 171, 177, 181, and 183; United Nations, Statistical Yearbook (Part 3) 1973, (New York: UN, 1973), pp. 31-35.

It is estimated that in the 1971/72 year about 20,000 new rural housing units were built. Urban housing needs in 1971/72 were estimated at 17,000 units per annum, for replacement as well as to solve the problems of overcrowding and new family formation. However, in that year about only 10,000 units were constructed.[28] Yet this would seem an impressive record when compared with the following 1961 partial figures for Tanganyika: 63 housing units for Dar es Salaam alone and 85 for other townships. Unfortunately, there are no current data available on the general situation of housing so it is difficult to know to what extent the housing problem has been solved.

Nevertheless, Table 5.6 reveals a humane approach to the problems of those in the lower income group who generally, in most other African countries, suffer most from the high cost of accommodation.

TABLE 5.6

Ratio of Monthly Income to Accommodation Costs in Tanzania, 1971-72

Income Group	Monthly Income per Household (shillings)	Percent Monthly Income Affordable for Rent
Low	0-500	10
Medium	500-1,000	11 plus
High	1,000-plus	15-25

Source: United Republic of Tanzania, Economic Survey 1971 - 72 (Dar es Salaam: Government Printer, 1973), p. 103.

Tanzania tries to respond to the housing needs of all its citizens as Table 5.6 demonstrates, and this is in line with her socialist program. Also in accordance with this program, the government provides free housing to a lot of the Tanzanian citizens, for example, the total value of free rations issued to employees in 1970 rose from T. Sh. 2.1 million in 1969 to T. Sh. 5.0 million in 1970; in the enterprise sector the value rose from T. Sh. 1.9 million in 1969 to T. Sh. 4.5 million in 1970; while in the public services sector it rose from T. Sh. 0.2 million to T. Sh. 0.5 million in 1970. The number of employees receiving free rations also rose from 8,297 in 1969 to 8,827 in 1970. Of this number, 805 were in the enterprise sector and 772 in the public services sector. The number of employees receiving free housing rose from 62,982 in 1969 to 72,349 in 1970.[29] With this review of social development in Tanzania we may want to know what economic progress has been made since the inception of independence in 1961.

Economic Development

In 1961 Tanzania's GDP at current prices was T. Sh. 3,870 million, of which agriculture alone was responsible for T. Sh. 2,282 million. The annual growth rate was 4.5 percent. In 1966 the GDP had risen to T. Sh. 5,444 million, of which agriculture alone was again responsible for T. Sh. 2,905 million. After the low growth rate in 1965 of just 1.2 percent, 1966 recorded 11.2 percent growth rate. In 1972 the GDP stood at T. Sh. 9,850 million, with agriculture still contributing a large share of T. Sh. 3,956 million.[30] The annual growth rate between 1964 and 1966 was 5 percent, in 1969-70 it was 6.6 percent, and 1970-71 it was 4.6 percent.[31]

On the whole the growth rate has been low, lower than the 6 percent considered appropriate by the World Bank for developing African countries. These figures are even more disappointing when they are seen in relation to the population growth rate of 2.8 percent over the same period. Thus the per capita GDP, which in 1964 was below $100, still remains just about the same by 1971 at $98.3, that is, an average growth rate in per capita GDP of 2.9 percent.[32]

However, we have indicated initially that Tanzania is naturally poor in mineral resources and that right from the day of independence she has had difficulties attracting foreign capital. This has caused Tanzania to adopt a policy of self-reliance, which culminated in the Arusha Declaration of 1967, a manifesto for African socialism. Since that time, too, development policies in the country have had different emphases, chief among which has been Ujamaa. It was for this reason that Tanzania nationalized all main financial institutions in order to redirect credit to the rural areas that constitute the backbone of the national economy.[33]

Nyerere himself has been realistic to admit that the fruits of rural socialism would not be visible until another one or two decades. However, in spite of this admission, and the fact that Tanzania has a very low per capita GDP and is one of the least developed countries in the African continent, the development concept itself has brought about some visible appreciable signs. For example, for the period 1966-69 (data beyond that period are not available) there was a decline in subsistence production as percentage of the GDP[34] This shows that the rural economy is being more and more monetized as the country is urbanized.

CONCLUSION

It does not matter whether it takes two or even three decades for the fruits of African socialism to be visible, ripe, and ready for distribution among the Tanzanians. Nyerere has succeeded in achieving what is still lacking in many other African countries: He has provided the Tanzanians with a systematic framework for development as well as a responsible leadership to guide the country toward attaining its development objectives. In this respect Tanzania was a leader because she was soon followed by such other African countries as Zambia and Uganda.

NOTES

1. J. K. Nyerere, Socialism and Rural Development (Dar es Salaam: Government Printer, 1967), p. 4.
2. J. K. Nyerere, Ujamaa: The Basis of African Socialism (Dar es Salaam: Tanganyika Standard, 1962), p. 6.
3. Nyerere, Socialism and Rural Development, op, cit., p. 11.
4. Ibid., p. 12.
5. Ibid., p. 16.
6. Ibid., p. 31.
7. TANU Constitution (Dar es Salaam: Mwanachi Publishing Co., 1962). (English translation, from TANU National Headquarters, mimeographed.)
8. For details, see Martin Minogue and Judith Molloy, eds., African Aims and Attitudes: Selected Documents (Cambridge: Cambridge University Press, 1974), p. 69.
9. Ibid., p. 76.
10. United Nations Statistical Yearbook (Part 3) 1973 (New York: UN, 1973), p. 31.
11. Eleazar Iwuju, "Report on Wage/Salary Structures in English-Speaking Africa" in ILO/DANIDA Regional Seminar on Wages, mimeographed (Geneva: ILO, November, 1974), p. 59.
12. See A. Baron Holmes IV, "The Committee on International Migration of Talent," in The International Migration of High-Level Manpower (New York: Praeger, 1970), p. 411.
13. Tanzania Statistical Abstract (Dar es Salaam: Government Printer, 1970), p. 201.
14. Ibid., pp. 217-19.
15. In J. K. Nyerere, Education for Self-Reliance (Dar es Salaam: Government Printer, 1967), p. 7.
16. Ibid., p. 14.
17. Guy Routh, "Development Paths in Tanzania," in Development Paths in Africa and China, Ukandi G. Damachi, et al., (London: Macmillan, 1970), Chapter 2.
18. J. K. Nyerere, Freedom and Socialism (Oxford: Oxford University Press, 1968), p. 351.
19. United Republic of Tanzania, Annual Plan for 1972/73 (Dar es Salaam: Government Printer, 1972), p. 51.
20. Routh, op. cit., p. 28.
21. Henry Bienen, Tanzania: Party Transformation and Economic Development (Princeton, N.J.: Princeton University Press, 1970), p. 251.
22. Fred Burke, "The Search for Ujamaa" in African Socialism, eds. William Friedland and Carl Rosenberg, Jr. (Stanford, Calif.: Stanford University Press, 1964), p. 219.

23. Bienen, op. cit., pp. 266-67.

24. International Monetary Fund, *Surveys of African Economies*, Vol. 2 (Washington, D.C.: IMF, 1970), pp. 237-38.

25. Manfred Bienefeld, "The Informal Sector and Peripheral Capitalism: The Case of Tanzania," *Human Resources Research* (Institute of Development Studies Bulletin) 6, no. 3 (February 1975): 56.

26. Bienen, op. cit., p. 212.

27. United Nations, *Statistical Yearbook (Part 3) 1973*, op. cit., pp. 31-38.

28. United Republic of Tanzania, *Economic Survey 1971-72* (Dar es Salaam: Government Printer, 1973), pp. 101-05.

29. United Republic of Tanzania, *Survey of Employment and Earnings 1970* (Dar es Salaam: Government Printer, 1972), p. 13.

30. United Nations, *Statistical Yearbook (Part 3) 1973*, op. cit., pp. 31-34.

31. United Nations, *Survey of Economic Conditions in Africa* (New York: UN, 1972), p. 46.

32. Ibid., p. 48.

33. John Lonsdale, "The Tanzanian Experiment," *African Affairs* 67, no. 269 (October 1968): 339.

34. United Nations, *Statistical and Economic Information Bulletin for Africa*, no. 6 (1971), p. 66.

CHAPTER

6

MARIEN N'GOUABI: SCIENTIFIC SOCIALISM IN THE CONGO

The territory of the People's Republic of the Congo, similiar in shape and size to Italy, stretches for almost 1,600 kilometers along the right bank of the Congo River and its tributary, the Oubangui. The country's colonial history is similar to that of the Ivory Coast. The Congo was part of French Equatorial Africa (AEF). Brazzaville, now the Congo's capital, was then the capital of the whole region. It became independent in 1960 with Abbe Youlo as its first president. He was overthrown in 1963 by Massemba-Debat who became the second president of the Republic. In September 1968, Massemba-Debat was also ousted by a military coup and Commandant N'Gouabi became president in December 1968.

In December 1969 the 1963 Constitution was abolished and a new Constitution, making the country a People's Republic, was proclaimed. The Congolese Workers' Party (Parti Congolais du Travail, PCT) and the State Council (Conseil d'Etat) became the major political institutions. The party is directed by the Political Bureau, consisting of 10 members, and the Central Committee, which is made up of 34 members. The president, who is automatically the head of the party, pledged when he was sworn in to be guided by "Marxist-Leninist principles." His development ideology is derived mainly from Marxist-Leninism.

SCIENTIFIC SOCIALISM

Unlike Kaunda, Nyerere, and Khama, who have been heavily influenced by the traditional African culture and organization in formulating their ideologies, N'Gouabi has been influenced by what he himself calls "colonial development" and the present international economic order or relations.

Colonial development, according to him, was characterized by the complete destruction of the national economy, until then relatively integrated—at least at the level of large regional entities. The result of this was, on the one hand, an axis from the Congo River to the sea front, equipped with the minimum necessary to satisfy the needs of the French economy, and on the other hand, an impoverished hinterland. Together these entities formed a reality totally unknown before colonization and quite incapable of favoring either the development of regions along the axis or of the hinterland, much less than of the whole country.

What is more, the present state of international economic relations, largely controlled by international imperialism, brings about and reinforces an unequal international specialization, which inevitably implies economic domination, technological dependence, a worsening of the terms of exchange, and so on. Consequently, economic development—which implies interdependence and integration of the different regions of the country, complementarity and solidarity of the diverse economic sectors, coherence, and, finally, autodynamism of the economic system—cannot absolutely be realized within the present Congolese social structure dominated by foreign capitalism. There is therefore an urgent need for a radical transformation of the present socioeconomic structures. N'Gouabi considers such a step an indispensable condition for economic development. In principle this step is incompatible with the "blind forces of laissez-faire economic system"[1] or capitalism. However, a transformation of this type can only come about through a fierce, organized struggle on the political, economic, social, and cultural levels, which demands an adequate politicoeconomic strategy. On the socioeconomic level, this organized struggle falls naturally within the framework of a centrally planned economy, or what he terms "scientific socialism."

But scientific socialism entails planning, which is an indispensable tool in the conquest of an independent national economy. To N'Gouabi the road to this scientific socialism is a rough one and thus it has to be traversed in stages.

The first stage, the "liquidation of the domination of foreign capital," involves the resolution of the principal contradiction that opposes the Congolese revolutionary forces against the reactionary forces comprising, in particular, French and international imperialism as well as their local allies, the bureaucratic bourgeoisie.[2] The revolutionary forces are composed of the working class, the peasants, and the intermediary (that is, the lower-middle class, youth and student movements). The most important undertaking at this stage is mass opposition by the Congolese people against foreign monopolistic capitalism, principally French imperialism, which is the most dominant in the country.

This opposition would hopefully facilitate the overthrow of the domination of the French imperialism and the eradication of the old

French colonial administrative machinery, which is to be replaced by a simple democratic administration entirely at the service of the people.[3]

The second stage is the "building of socialism," which is characterized by the national, democratic, and popular revolution. The revolution is called national because after the overthrow of the French imperialism the country would then be both politically and economically free. It is democratic because it attempts to substitute the dominion of the immense majority of the people for the domination of an infinitesimal minority. Finally, it is popular because it seeks to lay the economic, social, and cultural foundations of the next stage, which is the socialist revolution. This is due to come about by mobilizing the vast disinherited masses under the banner of the proletariat and its vanguard, the Congolese Workers' party.

Also, this stage of the national democratic and popular revolution entails not only economic independence but also the "socialization of the principal means of production"[4] by the party. The whole ideology is Lenin redivivus--very much like his New Economic Policy.[5]

In order to translate the ideology of scientific socialism into action, the party has set up some basic objectives:

1. Make agriculture the base and industry a determining factor. Agriculture is understood in a wider sense to include agriculture per se, fishing, forestry, and mining.
2. Begin to establish a harmonious equilibrium between the regions. Efforts are to be made to break down the existence of regions and enclaves in the hinterland, notably by the construction of suitable routes of communication.
3. Diminish social inequalities.
4. Encourage the national private sector in well-defined activities.
5. Carry on a policy of full employment with a view to liquidating unemployment.
6. Carry out an active campaign to stamp out illiteracy.
7. Develop basic health services into a system of preventive medicine for the popular masses as well as train medical personnel to meet present and future needs.[6]

PROGRAMS OF ACTION

In order to attain the above objectives the party has developed systematic programs. Since the national ideology is scientific socialism, there is a complete faith in development planning.

The government has drawn up a permanent development plan that embodies the basic development objectives. The plan aims at eventually harmonizing the two structures of the Congolese economy:

the foreign capitalist sector, still dominant, and the state sector, which is growing rapidly. Around these two sectors revolve the mixed sector and private national sector, still in its infancy.

The National Planning Council, a democratic institution largely representative of and formed by functionaries of the party and state, is charged with the responsibility of drawing up the plan and making sure that it is properly implemented. All its decisions are, however, subject to approval by the central communities. The work of the members of the council is nonremunerative.

In order to implement the plan various planning councils are set up at the regional and communal levels. These are composed of party members, technicians of the Ministry of Planning, and members of the "organization of masses." They meet once a year to prepare for the annual meeting of the National Planning Council.

Built into this structure is a mechanism of control that is political in nature:

> The Party, relying on its structures, the mass organizations, . . . and the existing State bodies will exercise permanent control over the implementation of the Plan. For this purpose, it will require, at all times, detailed reports and will carry out the necessary verification. An evaluation shall be presented to the National Council.[7]

With regard to the corpus of the plan, priority is given to the modernization of the countryside and the improvement in the living conditions of the working masses as well as the reinforcement of organization, instruction, and education of the peasant masses. The overall goals of the plan are the amelioration of and growth in the material and spiritual welfare of the Congolese citizens, the consolidation of independence, and the strengthening of the defense of the country.

On the whole, in the People's Republic of the Congo the plan is the affair of all the people and not the preserve of a handful of technocrats. Thus, under the direction and leadership of the party all active forces of the nation must participate in the conception, preparation, and implementation of the plan. The role of the party therefore consists of:

1. Perfecting its leadership and supervision machinery by which it can bring the base of the society to participate effectively at the local and regional levels;
2. Creating party cells in all places of work, but principally in the industrial enterprises, for it is precisely here that the leadership thinks the struggle must take place--the struggle for production and that for technological revolution;
3. Allowing members of the Party to exchange ideas freely and to educate themselves within the committees, branches and federations of the Party which are destined to become the vital centers for the interests of the workers in general. . . .[8]

The programs of action are aimed at involving every Congolese citizen in the development process. The next section will discuss to what extent the party has been able to implement these programs so as to attain its socialist objectives.

EVALUATION: ATTAINMENT OF DEVELOPMENT OBJECTIVES

Population

With regard to the labor force, the population of the Congo increased from 790,000 in 1960 (year of independence) to 1,100,000 in 1972. This means a modest growth rate of about 2.1 percent. In 1962 about 21.4 percent of the population lived in urban areas and by 1970 it had increased to 39 percent. In 1963/64 the economically active population was about 340,000 persons, 60 percent of whom were engaged in agriculture and forestry, 14 percent in crafts and commerce, and the rest in administrative and service sectors. The number of wage earners was estimated at 57,000 persons, that is, about 17 percent of the active population. Of these, 16,000 were in the public sector and 41,000 in the private.[9]

Education

The above figures show that the Congo, in comparison to the other African countries, is far more urbanized and has more people as wage earners. The reasons for this impressive showing are a result of various factors. The People's Republic of the Congo seems to have had one of the highest school attendance rates in all of Africa upon independence. Table 6.1 shows school enrolment in 1958, two years before independence.

TABLE 6.1

School Enrolment in the Congo, 1958

Levels	Number	Enrolment
Primary schools	482	78,962
Secondary schools	10	1,975
Technical schools	25	1,284

Note: The number of students studying abroad was 108.

Source: Violane Junod, ed., Handbook of Africa (New York: Columbia University Press, 1963), p. 73.

The school attendance meant that 72.2 percent of the children of school-going age attended school, of which 22.7 percent were girls. The importance placed on education at that early time is also reflected by the fact that 26.2 percent of the annual local budget was devoted to education.[10] By 1960, the number of primary schools had reached 495, while enrolment stood at 99,400 pupils. The 10 secondary schools had nearly doubled their intake to 3,370 students, while enrolment in 30 technical schools was 1,365 students. However, there was no university and the only institution for higher studies was the Center of Administrative and Advanced Technical Studies. In 1960, 214 students were enroled.[11]

In 1961, primary school enrolment had reached 135,000, while the percentage of school-age enrolment had increased to 75 percent and the population of girls had reached 30 percent of the total enrolment. The percentage of the annual budget devoted to education was still about 25.

By 1968-69 the country still had one of the highest levels of education in Africa. Education from 6 to 16 years became compulsary. In the same academic year primary school enrolment had jumped from the 1961 figure of 135,000 to 212,259 pupils, secondary-level students had increased to 21,800, while technical stood at 1,547. Enrolment at the Center for Advanced Studies was 1,100 students.[12]

It can be observed from the above figures that the progress of education after independence in 1960 has been very rapid and much attention continues to be paid to education in the annual budget, even after the adoption of scientific socialism as a development ideology by N'Gouabi. The credit is not due so much to his government as it is to the preceding governments, and even the French Colonial Government, which set the foundation for rapid educational development. Nevertheless, we need to acknowledge his foresight in continuing to expand and develop education as a prerequisite for the supply and utilization of the critical high-level and skilled manpower needed for development.

In spite of this emphasis on manpower supply and utilization, the country has thus far relied heavily on French and, since the overthrow of Massemba-Debat in 1968, Russian and Chinese experts. Specific statistics on the effect of high manpower shortages on the labor force are not available.

However, as previously indicated, although the Congolese educational system is one of the most advanced in Africa, the yearly output of teachers and university-level graduates is very small. Thus, as recently as 1970, 30 percent of the junior and over 80 percent of the senior secondary school teachers were expatriates. In 1974, whereas over 37,000 pupils were enroled in regular secondary schools, only 4,000 students were in technical and vocational institutions.[13]

Consequently, there seems to be a misemphasis in the educational structure since the country has a great shortage of technical talents. There seems to be too much concentration on training in socialist ideology. The overall effects of the shortage of technical and managerial manpower is that the manufacturing sector, on which the country heavily depends, is dominated by expatriates.

Labor Force and Employment

The same situation exists with respect to other professions, the only exception being law. For example, as recently as 1972, of the 91 doctors in the whole country, only 14 were Congolese.[14] Although there is no specific information as to what levels in each sector of the economy are occupied by Congolese or expatriates, Table 6.2 on the employment situation in 1968 is nonetheless indicative. The total

TABLE 6.2

Estimated Employment by Sector in the Congo at the End of 1968

Private (including state enterprises)	Congolese	Non Congolese African	Non-African
Manufacturing	12,379	196	315
Transport and communication	11,709	314	314
Agriculture and forestry	7,607	245	265
Construction and public works	6,737	60	187
Household services	6,000	--	--
Commerce	5,816	230	752
Services	3,082	63	311
Mining and quarrying	2,555	94	159
Electricity and water	823	32	43
Bank and insurance	611	22	107

Source: International Bank for Reconstruction and Development, The Economy of the People's Republic of Congo: Recent Evolution and Prospects, mimeographed, November 1971.

number of wage earners was about 80,000, of which about 61,000 were in the private sector, government services being about 19,000 or about 24 percent of the total wage-earning labor force. In numerical strength, not very many expatriates are employed in the private sector; and we may assume that the same situation applies in the public service. But the foreign predominance in the labor force is not a matter of sheer numbers, but of earning capacity and decision making. Although few in numbers, in the 1960s the expatriates occupied the top positions in industry and thus constituted not only the main decision makers, but also the top salary earners. For example, in 1967 expatriate wage earners (about 5 percent of the total employment) took 30 percent of the total wage bill of CGAG 10.9 billion. This was nonetheless a decrease from a share of 57 percent in 1958.

Also with N'Gouabi's ideology of scientific socialism, which aims at a radical indigenization of the economy, it may be concluded that this percentage has further decreased. There are no available statistics to substantiate this claim, however, Does this mean then that N'Gouabi is succeeding in attaining the ideals of his socialist ideology, that is, of "seizing control of the national economy from French and international imperialism" and of guaranteeing that the average Congolese citizen benefits from his country's development?

Economic Development

In order to answer this question we first need to review the history of economic development in the country, which has been affected significantly by two factors. Before the country became independent in 1960 it was a member of French Equatorial Africa (AEF) and Brazzaville served as the administrative capital of the federation. As a result the country benefited a great deal from providing administrative and other services for member states. Incomes derived from these services accounted for a large part of the GDP. Moreover, it enjoyed having the federation as a large market for its manufacturing industry. But with independence the federation was dissolved and with it the Congo lost its political and economic status in the region. In 1966 when the Cameroons entered the region's Customs Union—Union Douaniere et Economique de l'Afrique Centrale (UDEAC) the economic prospects for the Congo were further altered because it now had to face greater competition from the Cameroons in the field of manufacturing and commerce. However, throughout the late 1960s the economy performed adequately well.

In 1968, when Marien N'Gouabi became president after a successful military coup, the country, as we have previously noted, turned Marxist and this meant heavy state involvement in the economy. Although the involvement has paid off in many aspects, nonetheless, the economy seems to have been on the slide since the 1969/70 period as the figures for the growth of GDP and per capita incomes would indicate.[15]

In spite of the increasing importance of manufacturing and industry and a fast rate of urbanization, economically the Congo is still an agrarian country. Although agriculture, fishing, and forestry accounted for only 13 percent of the GDP in 1967 (in 1958 they accounted for only 13 percent), they not only provide for about 60 percent of the country's total export, they also provide a living for about 60 percent of the population. However, since independence the manufacturing and services sectors have grown very rapidly and both have contributed to the strength of the economy.

The GDP has shown a steady increase since independence but it is beginning to decrease considerably under the N'Gouabi administration. In 1958 the GDP was CFAF 23 billion, but this had increased to CFAF 34.2 billion by 1963 and to CFAF 59 billion in 1967. This means that between 1958 and 1967 the GDP had increased at the annual rate of 11 percent, which is quite impressive.

This impressive performance declined when the country became socialist under N'Gouabi's leadership. In 1969 the GDP was $240 million and by 1971 it had slightly declined to $235 million. Some of the reasons that might have accounted for this decline could have been the euphoria that the working class exhibited with the changeover from a capitalist to a socialist economy. Such a dramatic change could have resulted in a decrease in productivity and hence a fall in the GDP. Also, the implementation of scientific socialism implies a radical replacement of high-level expatriate personnel with even mediocre nationals who might not have been experienced in production and management techniques.

Whatever reason might have been responsible for the decline in economic performance was also responsible for the fall in the per capita income, which previously was on the increase. For example, in 1963 the per capita GDP was about $265. By 1970 it declined to $250.50 and in 1971 it went further down to $247.10 (at constant market prices).[16]

Health Services

The implementation of scientific socialism has not brought about substantive improvement in health services either. In 1958 the Congo had only one major hospital. There were, however, 13 medical centers, 20 infirmaries, 69 dispensaries, and 27 private institutions. These were manned by 95 physicians, making the number of inhabitants per doctor to be 8,000, which is quite impressive compared to either Zambia or the Ivory Coast. At independence there were still only two large hospitals in the country, one in Brazzaville and another in Point-Noire, 13 medical centers, 20 infirmaries, and 78 dispensaries. The number of doctors was still 95 but they were assisted by over 700 nurses.[17]

By 1972, when N'Gouabi had been in power for nearly four years, there were only 2 large hospitals, 17 medical centers, 182 dispensaries, 25 infirmaries, 11 maternity clinics, 1 tuberculosis clinic, and 37 health centers. The number of personnel had changed for the worse, reflecting the preponderance of expatriates despite the objective of getting rid of "imperialism and its vestiges" from the country. Indeed, the number of doctors was now 91, out of which only 14 were Congolese and the number of inhabitants per doctor was now 11, 000, a poor performance when compared to that of the Youlou and Massemba-Debat governments.

CONCLUSION

On the whole, although the ideals of scientific socialism, from the evidence presented above, seem far from being realized, it is encouraging that the N'Gouabi Government has at least been able to provide a framework and direction for the country's development. The government needs to follow this direction with more realistic programs aimed at solving some of the key national problems of development such as the critical manpower shortage and the lack of adequate health facilities. It is too early to judge the success of scientific socialism in the People's Republic of the Congo; but the actions of the N'Gouabi Government tend to demonstrate that it means business.

NOTES

1. People's Republic of the Congo, Directives of the Central Committee of the Congolese Workers' Party for the Planning of Social and Economic Development in the Popular Republic of the Congo, mimeographed (Brazzaville: Government Printer, 1973), p. 2.
2. People's Republic of the Congo, Programme du Parti Congolais du Travail (Brazzaville: Government Printer, 1973), p. 25.
3. Ibid., p. 26.
4. Ibid., pp. 24-25.
5. For an elaborate discussion of this policy, see Anatole G. Mazour, Soviet Economic Development: Operation Outstrip 1921-1965 (Princeton, N.J.: D. Van Nostrand, 1967), pp. 21-33.
6. People's Republic of the Congo, Programme de Parti Congolais du Travail, op. cit., p. 8; and Directives of the Central Committee of the Congolese Workers' Party, op. cit., pp. 16-19.
7. People's Republic of the Congo, Programme de Parti Congolais du Travail, op. cit., p. 23.
8. Ibid., pp. 8-9.
9. International Monetary Fund, Surveys of African Economies, Vol. 1 (Washington, D. C.: IMF, 1970), p. 230.
10. Violane Junod, ed., Handbook of Africa (New York: Columbia University Press, 1963), p. 73.

11. France, Member States of the French Community (Paris: Government Printer, 1961), pp. 16-18.

12. Africa Annual Review, 1972 (London: Africa Journal Ltd.), p. 110.

13. Europa, Africa South of the Sahara, 1974 (London: Europa Publications, 1974), p. 258.

14. Africa Annual Review, op. cit., p. 110.

15. Europa, Africa South of the Sahara, op. cit., p. 253.

16. IMF, Surveys of African Economies, Vol. 1, op. cit., p. 230

17. France, Member States of the French Community, op. cit., p. 18.

CHAPTER

7

MO'AMMAR AL-GADHAFI: ARAB-ISLAMIC SOCIALISM IN LIBYA

The history of "modern" Libya began in 1951. We use the word "modern" to distinguish between the only two periods in its national history in which Libya enjoyed independence. The first period of independence began in 1200 B. C. after a long spate of domination by various invaders and ended in 900 B. C. From that period the country was again subjected to various invasions and occupations until Turkey finally became the unchallenged ruler in 1551. Turkish rule was terminated with the Turkish-Italian War and the defeat of the former in 1911. From then on, Libya was once more subjugated incessantly to various foreign powers, each for a short period of time. The Italians occupied the country from 1911 to 1939, then with the outbreak of World War II the British defeated the Italians and occupied Libya, only for the British in the same year to be defeated by German troops. Two years later the British recaptured the Libyan territory, only again to lose it soon after to the Italians and Germans. In 1943 the British (under the leadership of Montgomery) and the French drove out the Italians and Germans and thereupon took effective control of Libya, each occupying different parts of the country. It was not until eight years later, after the 1949 United Nations' resolution, that Libya finally gained independence for a second time under King Idris I.

We have given a brief history of Libya to emphasize one point in our discussion of the country's development since independence: This is that Libya was a "colonial" territory but not in the strict sense we understand the term when we discuss other African countries that had been subjugated to foreign rule. The long Moslem Turkish occupation had merely reinforced the Muslim culture and tradition of the country, but there is hardly any evidence that the Turks had attempted to develop Libya into a modern state. Not only did Turkey seem to lack the financial and technological resources, but Libya was too vast and too poor to be considered an economically viable state. Again, except perhaps under the Italians, there was little time, and maybe desire, on the part of occupying powers after 1911 to set up administrative or economic machinery with a view to developing the country. Thus when Libya finally became independent in 1951 there was hardly a question of building on a colonial administrative or economic infrastructure. We may also point out that these historical factors helped shape Gadhafi's development ideology.

THE THIRD INTERNATIONAL THEORY: ARAB-ISLAMIC SOCIALISM

The theory is a mix of Gadhafi's political and socio-economic attitudes to Arab nationalism as a whole and Libyan development in particular. Since the main theme of this book is on the African leaders' socioeconomic attitudes toward development, we shall center our discussion only at this level.[1]

The Third International Theory is based on Islam, in its divine and nonfanatical concept. The rationale for basing the theory on Islam is that it "is a religion that provides answers to every minute question whether it is earthly or spiritual."[2] It is because of this aspect of Islam, Gadhafi contends, that the Libyan Arab Republic has dedicated itself to the benefit of truth, freedom, and peace in the world.

But the most important aspect of freedom is social justice and equity. In practice these two concepts mean "emancipation of the society from poverty by providing every citizen with bread and butter (if possible jam) and by preventing the exploitation of one citizen by another."[3] This in principle is socialism.

Thus this type of socialism, which is derived from Islam, prohibits any rich person from using his wealth as an instrument of oppression. It puts a limitation on ownership of property by authorizing the state to either nationalize or expropriate excessive wealth through progressive income tax or any other suitable measures when such wealth is deemed misused. However, property may continue to be free if it causes no harm. Gadhafi then tends to contradict himself by postulating that "wealth and property should not be allowed to coexist in one society."[4] In case this happens the government is entitled to enact relevant laws that would provide "for taking away from the rich and giving to the poor."[5] But is it possible for a wealthy person to refrain from having property?

In summary, the central tenets of Arab-Islamic socialism, as enunciated by Gadhafi himself, are as follows:

> Our Socialism differs from the imperialist and communist versions of social justice. Our Socialism is derived from our own heritage and responds to the needs of our Society. It serves mankind, gives human being his due importance, protects him from exploitation of class in whatsoever form

> it may be. Our Socialism denies the validity of communism and imperialism. It derives the concept from Islam. It guarantees the right to personal property. It believes in the union of the working class of the society without allowing any class to exploit another. It believes in human values and condemns communist denial of religion.[6]

To Gadhafi his socialist ideology is not an end in itself, instead it is a means for the achievement of benefit and happiness of man. Accordingly, he considers the individual as key to government development policies and programs. In this regard he pointed out that "we cannot crush the individual for the sake of the class and in order to build a socialist society."[7]

For Islamic socialism to succeed, it has to develop a deep sense of nationalism among the Libyans and/or Arabs as a whole. Gadhafi regards such Arab nationalism as a call for peace, prosperity, and progress. It is appropriate to ask at this stage what steps has Gadhafi taken to put his ideology into operation.

PROGRAMS OF ACTION

Since his ideology aims at seeking solutions to Libya's economic problems and at improving the living standards of the Libyan citizens through socialism, a new and pioneering program is being launched in the country. People's committees have been set up in every village, oasis, city, school, and university. These committees entitle the masses to govern themselves along socialist lines.

Economic establishments, insurance companies, and the British Petroleum Company have been nationalized. There has been a revision of all existing laws in accordance with Islamic laws and of agricultural policies. Also, socialist ordinances (a ban on exploitation of manual labor, doubling of workers' wages) have been instituted.

Moreover, the Arab Socialist Union has been set up to protect the freedom of the Libyan citizens. It should be pointed out that the union is to seek ways and means to bring about a unification of Libya and Egypt. Gadhafi believes strongly that a successful implementation of these programs of action would lead to "a true expression of Arabism, humanitarianism, socialism, and progress."[8] To what extent have the programs been implemented?

EVALUATION: PERFORMANCE OF THE DEVELOPMENT IDEOLOGY

Population

According to the 1954 census, the population of Libya was 1, 089, 000; by 1964 it had jumped to 1, 559, 399. This means that within that ten-year period the population increased by 470, 000, an increase of over 43 percent. In mid-1972 the population was estimated to be 2, 096, 000, which means an annual rate of growth of 3.7 percent between 1964 and 1972.[9] By UN standards the growth rate was extremely high.

With regard to the labor force participation in 1964 the economically active population was 405, 258. The number of aliens in the labor force was 17, 559. By 1967 there were 41, 200 aliens, or 9.7 percent of the work force. In 1968 the economically active population was 465, 700, or approximately 25 percent of a total population estimated at 1.8 million that year.[10] The average growth rate of aliens in the labor force in this period, 1964-68, was 13.4 percent while that of the nationals was only 3.2 percent. The aliens, therefore, had a predominance in the labor force. What gave rise to this predominance?

Education

To answer this question, we shall examine the development of education and manpower training in Libya before and after independence. We have indicated that the invading powers who had subjugated Libya to foreign rule for centuries had done little or nothing to develop the country. Regarding education, what had happened had been one continuous process of change and cancellation. First the Arabs came, ruled, and established the religion of Islam.

Throughout their long rule, the Turks did nothing about education and the Libyans were left to rely on the mosques or so-called Koranic schools. They learned to recite the Koran and maybe also learned religion and Arabic grammar, but nothing else. Even the centers where these subjects were taught were exceedingly few and were to be found only in Tripolitania or the northeastern part of the country around Tripoli. Toward the middle of the nineteenth century, however, the Sanusi Order,* in an attempt to stimulate religions and secular

*For many years religion in Libya had felt the influence of the Sanusi movement, founded in the mid-nineteenth century by the scholar Sayid Mohammad bin Ali al Sanusi, to reform and spread Islam and free it from the non-Muslim practices that had developed among the unschooled. This became popularly known as the Sanusi Order.

education, established various houses of worship and learning, or "Zawaayaa," all over the country and founded an Islamic university at Al Saghbub where Zawiya Sheiks were trained.[11] The main purpose of the Islamic University and the Zawaayaa, admittedly, was to perceive and foster the country's Islamic heritage and Arab culture.

The Turks during their long period of rule were as indifferent to questions of education, especially the Koranic schools, as they had been to other matters of development. The only measures taken about education were merely to serve the needs of the administrators and military personnel. Consequently, during their rule of Libya, the Koranic schools declined.

The Libyans had no idea of modern education until the arrival of the Italians, who closed down most of the Zawaayaa and instead built a number of schools all over the country, even in the most remote parts of the Fezzan. But again these schools were not established to train Libyan skills but to teach Italian language and culture "to plant Italian principles and ideas and kill Libyan nationalism."[12] The policy of colonial administration, as often was the case, was to restrict the number of Libyans educated beyond the first grade. Libyans were almost always excluded from attending private Italian secondary schools unless, of course, they obtained Italian citizenship and had a reading knowledge of the Italian language, since classes were taught in Italian.

We pointed out, while discussing Botswana, that most Africans kept their children away from school because of their fears that Western education would subvert the community's traditions and values. Although during the 1930s the Libyan school population was allowed to expand, many Libyan parents kept their children away from school for fear of exposing them to foreign influences that might weaken their Islamic faith and undermine the Muslim way of life. Even worse, it has been argued that the reason parents refused to send their children to school was because of threats and campaigns against Western education by the Koranic teachers who feared the loss of their livelihood since they depended on the weekly donations of their pupils.[13] Nonetheless, in all cases, children were urged to go to the Koranic schools where they were given tradition and religious education.

The British further expanded the educational system by establishing secondary and technical schools. But again these were to be found only in the coastal areas.

Thus, on the eve of independence in 1951 only 537 of the total school population of 32,741 were attending secondary and technical schools. The number of secondary school teachers was 25 and only 14 Libyans had university degrees. The illiteracy rate was about 90 percent.[14]

After independence, education was not only accelerated but drastically overhauled along Arab-Islamic socialist principles. Although during the last decade of Italian rule primary school enrolment more than quadrupled, Libya felt that the Italian and British education which she had been compelled to adopt did not reflect the needs and values of the country. Thus, immediately after independence, when education became a major government responsibility, the focus was not only on accelerating the production of much-needed educated manpower but also on overhauling the educational system itself to reflect what the government regarded as the "Arab-Libyan spirit" and to preserve the best of the past traditions while eliminating what was inimical to the national progress.[15] It was for this reason that the University of Libya was established in 1955, just three years after independence.

To imbue the educational system with distinctly Arab values, the country had turned to Egypt. Libya not only adopted the Egyptian educational system and curriculum, she depended on Egypt to send teachers and books. Senior school examinations were supervised and corrected by Egyptians and even the results were announced from Egypt. It was not until 1957 that responsibility for the secondary school system was taken over by the newly established University of Libya. The new educational system stressed not only the theoretical part, that is, the one that leads through a secondary school and then into the university, it also emphasized the vocational and religious aspects.[16]

This brief account of the direction of the Libyan educational system immediately before and after independence is significant because it indicates that Libya is one, perhaps the only, country in modern Africa that upon independence has truly revamped the colonial educational system to suit not only its industrial needs but also its educational life.

Full details of educational progress in Libya immediately after independence are not available, but the following statistics will give us some general idea.

In Cyrenaica in 1951-52 there were 60 elementary and secondary schools (secondary could be preparatory teacher training, technical, and vocational). Within this period there were 8, 901 students in elementary schools and only 198 in secondary schools. During 1964-65 the numbers increased dramatically; 44, 063 elementary school students and 6, 843 secondary.[17]

There were similar improvements in other provinces. For example, in Tripolitania for the 1950-51 period there were 134 elementary schools and 2 secondary schools. The numbers of students in the elementary and secondary schools were 23, 188 and 414, respectively. By 1964-65 these numbers had improved to 115, 991 elementary school students and 16, 347 secondary.[18]

Fezzan, another province, had only 17 elementary schools with 1, 001 students in 1953. By 1964-65 there were 68 elementary schools with an enrolment of 9, 137. The region had its first secondary school in 1953 and enrolment stood at 88.[19]

In all of the three regions of Libya then, the 211 elementary schools and two secondary schools in 1951-53 had jumped to 735 and 142 respectively, by 1964-65. And the enrolment in 1951-53 zoomed from 33, 090 elementary school pupils and 612 secondary school pupils to 169, 191 and 23, 278, respectively, by 1964-65.[20] In 1964 there were 4, 750 secondary school certificate holders, 15, 954 intermediate school certificate holders, and 34, 499 primary school graduates.[21] This means that in the first decade of independence, school enrolment in the elementary level rose more than five times, while that in the secondary level more than quadrupled. This record is even more outstanding when it is remembered that only a mere 537 students had attended all forms of secondary school on the eve of independence. We have also indicated earlier that, by 1951, there were only 14 Libyans with university degrees, obtained mainly from Egyptian universities. In 1961, Libya had 318 students studying abroad in addition to the 1, 936 that had enroled at the University of Libya. By 1964 there were 1, 523 Libyan nationals with university degrees in the labor force. By the 1971/72 academic year (the Islamic University had by now been merged with the University of Libya) there were 6, 312 students enroled at the university. Of this number, 5, 315 were Libyan nationals. In the same academic year the number of students enroled in secondary schools (including preparatory) had reached 62, 618 and that of elementary was 407, 805.[22]

To summarize the situation Libya was in at the inception of independence, a quote from the World Bank Mission to Libya in 1969, that is, seven years after independence, is appropriate:

> It must be recognized, however, that the Libyans paid heavily for what the Italians achieved. They were pushed off some of the best farming land in the country; large numbers of their livestock were lost in the fighting (especially in Cyrenaica) and their traditional industries suffered severely from competition from Italian products. Moreover, the Italians did little or nothing to prepare the Libyans for self-government. Education and technical training were neglected and the Libyans were virtually excluded from the administration. As a result, through no fault of its own, Libya has remained heavily dependent on foreign administrative and technical personnel, and the training of Libyans to replace them is still the most difficult of all problems associated with economic development.[23]

Labor Force and Employment

Nevertheless, the vast educational reforms described above have begun to influence manpower development and utilization in the country.

In our summary of the history of Libya leading to her independence in 1951 we have indicated that it was a vast and very poor country and that universal opinion at the time was that it would be decades, if at all, before Libya could develop a viable economy. This was because Libya is about 85 percent desert, and at the time of independence, the country had no mineral resources. Agricultural and animal husbandry accounted for about 93 percent of the country's total output and between 75 and 85 percent of the entire Libyan labor force. The other 15 percent were mainly involved in exports and trade. There were hardly any industries except small plants for olives and olive oils and tanning.[24]

Labor-force figures for the years immediately before and after independence are not available, but it could be assumed that the pre-independence situation did not change much, if at all, soon after 1951. However, we have indicated that in 1964 the economically active population was estimated to be 405,258, including 17,559 aliens. By 1968 this had risen to 465,700. The 1964 figure coincides with the mining of petroleum that had begun in 1961.* The 1968 figure could thus be said to follow the expansion of the petroleum sector in between the years. By 1974 the labor force (excluding children below 15) was estimated to have reached 498,248 (including aliens)—an increase of over 110,000 over the 1964 figure.

In 1964 the percentage of Libyans in the total labor force involved in agriculture had dwindled to about 35 percent, 54 percent being now employed in mining and quarrying, manufacturing, construction, electricity and allied services, commerce, transport, and communication and general services. As estimated in the Second National Development Plan 1969-74 although the number of those in agriculture was expected to climb up from the 1964 figures of 136,389 to 159,439 by 1974 the percentage seemed to have gone down further to 32 percent.[25] This dramatic shift from agriculture to the modern sector from the independence period to 1964 and from then to 1974 is said by Nair to reflect the flow of workers from rural to urban centers because of high wages and perhaps also the availability of jobs in the modern sector.

The alien labor force was about 17,500 in 1964, or about 4.3 percent of the total labor force, and it is estimated that between 1954 and 1964 it grew by only 3.4 percent. By 1967 it had reached 41,200 or 9.7 percent of the work force. This increase was due mainly to the expansion of the oil industry, which brought in many foreign technicians and personnel. Assuming that by 1974 the growth remained steady or even slightly declined because of the government's tighter control of immigration of foreign workers into the country, this ratio of aliens to the overall labor force would still be regarded as large. However, if we compare the 1964 figures of wage earners in Libya with those

---

*The 1964 figure is said to include children below the age of 15, about 2.2 percent of the quoted figure, which were said to be economically active.

of other African countries (for example, Botswana's 48,000 out of a total population of over 500,000) we notice that the ratio of wage earners in Libya to the total labor force was exceedingly high. This conclusion is by no means an apologia for the predominance of alien labor force in the modern sector.

A further look at the employment picture in the country would demonstrate the extent of this foreign dominance and the chronic shortage of indigenous manpower. For example, in 1964 Libyan nationals formed only 7 percent of the 400 physicians and surgeons working in the country. By 1967 when the number had risen to 606 still only 39 were Libyans. In fact, it is estimated that in 1967 over 68 percent of all professional and managerial positions and about 22 percent of the intermediate-level technical jobs were held by aliens.[26] Out of about 5,400 workers employed by firms in petroleum and mining, in 1969 only 3,700 were Libyans.[27] Also in order to implement development plans, it was predicted that between 1968 and 1973, 3,800 foreign workers were needed annually. This was in spite of the fact that the government, since the late 1960s, had adopted the policy of insisting that all Libyan employees must be trained in the operation of whatever foreign concerns in which they happened to be employed.

Even to improve agriculture, on which Libya had depended until the discovery of oil in 1963, the government had had to rely on foreign teachers to provide the Libyans with the technical know-how. For example, in the 1950-51 academic year there were only 89 students in training institutes; however, by 1962-63 this had increased to 1,919.[28] The demand for technical manpower increased with the sudden wealth from petroleum and the consequent unanticipated boom in the economy in 1963. Libya needed 1,861 technicians between 1964 and 1969, but in 1963 all technical institutions in the country could produce only 182.

As a result the country had to plan to import 2,000 craftsmen yearly to meet its most basic needs. The yawning gulf between demand and supply existed in all categories of the labor force.[29] This unanticipated manpower pressure, combined with the easy availability of resources from petroleum, compelled King Idris's government to embark on ambitious expansion of the educational system to accelerate the production of urgently needed skilled manpower. By 1967-68 the government efforts seemed to have only very slightly paid off, but with the arrival of Gadhafi in the Libyan political arena the payoff has increased.

Economic Development

Before we go on to analyze Gadhafi's contribution in the area of social development, we need to have an idea of Libya's economic picture from independence to the present. We will then be in a better position to evaluate his contribution.

The foreign dominance in Libya was not only restricted to the area of employment, it was felt more in the control of the national economy.

Like Botswana, at independence Libya was considered economically unviable. Not only was 85 percent of the country desert, it lacked any mineral resources and thus it was considered that to improve the agricultural sector alone she would need foreign technical and financial assistance for many years. There was also the belief that even the modest budget that was being balanced with foreign aid would continue to be so for many years. It was therefore not surprising that Libya's economic prospects were deemed so hopelessly bleak that in 1951 UN experts characterized the country as the world's poorest nation.[30]

We have already indicated that at independence about 93 percent of Libya's output was in the form of agricultural products and that agriculture engaged between 75 and 85 percent of the total labor force. Agriculture accounted for about 30 percent of the total GDP, which was estimated at about £15 million.* By 1959, however, the GDP had climbed to some £56 million, or about $120 million. By then, too, the portion of the GDP contributed by agriculture had declined to 24.5 percent.[31]

In the late 1950s the GDP stagnated, but in 1961 came the petroleum miracle. Income derived from petroleum that year was about £4 million, accounting for about 7.5 percent of the total GDP. But in 1962 income from petroleum rose to about £125 million, accounting for 98.7 percent of the total value of Libyan domestic export. In 1969 oil revenue had reached well over $1.1 billion and in 1972 it was estimated to be twice as much. The increase in government oil revenues in the ten-year period between 1962 and 1972 represented a tenfold increase in GDP at current prices. By November 1973, after the great OPEC (Organization of Petroleum Exporting Countries) oil price increase, the income from petroleum had rocketed to $9.339 billion.[32]

However, as petroleum revenues increased income from nonpetroleum products declined precipitously. In 1966 mining and quarrying accounted for 57.5 percent of total domestic output, while agriculture declined to 4.6 percent. By 1970 Libya had moved from the "world's poorest country" to an affluent society.

But who controls the Libyan economy? Since Libya is generally assumed to have had no significant economy until the discovery and exportation of oil, we could safely talk about "control" starting with the period beginning in 1961. At that time King Idris ruled Libya. He was staunchly pro-Western and Libya thus had a laissez-faire economic policy. Right from the time that foreign companies descended on Libya for oil prospecting, the country had a dual economy—petroleum and nonpetroleum. The two economies operated side by side. The nonpetroleum economy was controlled by the king's government and the petroleum by

---

*One Libyan pound equals $2.10

the oil companies. Decisions affecting the activities of the petroleum were taken by the oil companies without regard to, or consideration for, the nonpetroleum.

The initial exploration of oil was begun by Esso in the late 1950s. By 1969 the number of companies holding concessions in Libya had reached 33. However, the majority of these and the bulk of the money that went into exploration activities were American. The laws that governed these activities were designed to attract foreign capital for exploration and production as rapidly as possible and were therefore very liberal and favorable to the oil companies. Until Libya joined OPEC in 1962, and even shortly after, she had allowed her oil companies to market their oil abroad at discounts from posted prices. The oil companies had tried unsuccessfully to make the other producing countries to follow the Libyan practice. The countries argued rather convincingly that such a move would reduce their revenues but increase the profits of the oil companies. As a result, OPEC put pressure on Libya to revise the exploration laws. She gave in by passing legislation in 1968 to stabilize posted prices of her petroleum.

In 1968 Libya created her own national oil company--the Libyan National Petroleum Company--which soon began to participate in the exploration, production, processing, and marketing aspects of the petroleum industry. From then on, too, the national oil company was authorized to establish a tanker fleet, to participate in the petrochemical industry, to represent the government in the control and supervision of the foreign petroleum companies. The government no longer gave concessions to foreign companies for unilateral exploration and exploitation as in the past. By 1969 the government had entered arrangements with various foreign companies to jointly operate some significant activities of the petroleum industry. Such was the state of the oil industry under King Idris.

Then enters Gadhafi. When Gadhafi came to power in 1969, after the overthrow of King Idris and the abolition of the monarchy, the oil industry underwent another dramatic change. Gadhafi was out to restructure the national economy along his ideology of Arab-Islamic socialism. By late 1969, therefore, Libya had entered arrangements with Algeria to team together to engage in all branches of petroleum exploration, production, marketing, and transportation as well as in the petrochemical industry. This first act was to indicate the socialism, nationalism, and pan-Arabism that were to become his guiding principles of petroleum policy making.

In the first year of her revolution, Libya increased the posted prices as a means of getting a greater share in oil company profits. In 1971 the government decreed that all foreign personnel in administrative and technical positions in foreign oil companies be replaced with Libyans. In 1970 Libya had nationalized the marketing subsidiaries of the foreign oil companies. She also insisted on majority partnership or total takeover of the joint projects the earlier government had entered into with foreign oil companies. Toward the end of 1971 nationalization of the oil companies themselves had begun.

It is clear from the preceding government action that Libya, which under King Idris in the early 1960s had been an enfant terrible in OPEC, had moved by the early 1970s to a position of leadership in challenging foreign domination in the oil industries of OPEC and in asserting the rights of nations to control their natural wealth.[33]

What is significant is that Gadhafi, intensifying the trend begun by King Idris, had succeeded by the early 1970s in merging the two hitherto separate economies of Libya, thereby laying the foundation for promoting Libyan nationalism.

Under Gadhafi, Libya's crusade for control of her economy has, of course, not been limited to petroleum. When Gadhafi came into power in 1969, to avenge the Italian occupation of 1911 - 39 he confiscated all Italian property in Libya—farms, and wholesale and retail firms. He nationalized all banking and insurance institutions. By 1972 Libya embarked on a program of modernization along socialist principles.

It is, of course, to be assumed that the radicalization of the economy, especially the nationalization of its important sectors and the introduction of ambitious projects, will severely tax the country's already scarce human resources. But with her surplus capital everything is within the realm of possibility.

Social Development

But is the Libyan benefiting from the country's economic miracle? To answer this question, we shall review the type of social development that has been taking place in Libya since independence. The meteoric rise in national income, of course, meant a consequent jump in per capita income. At independence when total GDP stood at about £15 million (or some $42 million), the per capita income was estimated to be about £11 (or $30). In 1958 it had risen to £40 (or $112). By 1964, when oil had begun to flow, per capita income more than quadrupled to $459, reaching $772 in 1966. The annual compounded rate of growth of per capita GDP between 1958 and 1966 was 26.2 percent. In 1968 per capita GDP stood at an estimated $1,839.[34] Figures for the years since October 1973 when oil prices quadrupled are not yet available but we can assume that, with greatly increased revenue from oil, the per capita GDP of the Libyan had reached another phenomenal height.

But in spite of the miraculous rise in wealth and calculated GDP, Libya is still far from being an egalitarian society. The distribution of income is still very uneven. Many Libyans still live on incomes far below the average, and while a few have become super-rich, a majority have achieved only a minimum standard of living.[35] In fact, it is estimated that 10 percent of the population receives 50 percent of the national income. While between 1964 and 1969 the GNP increased by 289 percent,[36] the income of the bottom 90 percent (and this is certainly a heavy "bottom") of the population increased by only 90 percent. Information for the period 1969 to the present is not available; as a result, we do not know whether the situation has improved since Libya became a socialist country under Gadhafi. However, it is clear from the development budgets of the 1972-75 years that Libya has embarked on projects that will give the ordinary Libyan a greater sense of participation in the sharing of national prosperity. Among these projects are health facilities, the provision of good housing, and the campaign against illiteracy.

As regards health, we have indicated that in 1967 Libya had 606 physicians and surgeons (a majority of whom were foreigners) working in the country. This means that between 1960 and 1967 the number of doctors increased 2.5 times. By 1971 the government is said to have had on contract 621 doctors in addition to many other foreign doctors in practice. In that same year seven new hospital projects were embarked upon to increase the number of beds. In 1972 plans for another 1,200-bed hospital were announced. It is to be remembered that in 1955 Libya had only 23 hospitals with a total of 2,825 hospital beds--400 inhabitants per bed. Tables 7.1 and 7.2 demonstrate the progress that Libya has made in health since independence. From these tables we can observe that Libya has made substantial progress in the area of health over the years, so much so that in 1971 the number of inhabitants per doctor stood at 3,100, a decrease from the figure of 10,000 in 1955, and the number of inhabitants per hospital bed was 314, down

TABLE 7.1

Number of Hospital Personnel in Libya, 1955-71

Year	Midwives	Pharmacies	Dentists	Physicians and Surgeons
1955	28	30	6	107
1965	76	57	36	409
1969	184	166	62	733
1971	304	111	76	1,041

Source: Libyan Arab Republic, Statistical Abstract, 1971 (Tripoli: Government Printer, 1972), p. 69.

TABLE 7.2

Health Facilities in Libya, 1955-71
(hospitals and health centers)

Year	Bed Capacity	Number of Hospitals and Health Centers
1955	2,825	23
1962	4,155	32
1967	5,786	43
1969	6,434	44
1971	8,457	80

Source: Libyan Arab Republic, Statistical Abstract, 1971 (Tripoli: Government Printer, 1972), pp. 70-71.

from the 1955 figure of 400. The figures are more impressive when compared to those of other North African countries: In the same period the number of inhabitants per doctor in Algeria was 5,000; Egypt, 3,000; Morocco, 9,500; and Tunisia, 7,000.[37]

Nonetheless, problems still abound in the area of health in Libya. As recently as 1971, average life expectancy was still 37 years and the infant mortality rate was an astonishing 300 per 1,000 live births.[38]

The housing situation has so far shown only marginal improvement. We might start our survey of the housing situation by looking at the housing figures in Table 7.3.

TABLE 7.3

Housing Situation in Libya, 1954

Type of Housing	Number of Households
Villas	6,312
Houses	115,658
Tents	51,939
Shanties	57,638
Caves	5,468
Improvised	1,812
Vessels	13
Collectives	819

Source: Rawle Farley, Planning for Development in Libya: The Exceptional Economy in the Developing World (New York: Praeger, 1971), p. 107.

The table indicates that in 1954 of a total 239,653 households, only 121,970 lived in adequate houses, the other half living in tents, shanties, and so on. It is, of course, to be assumed that with the increase in national and personal incomes the situation must have begun to change. But since independence the government has paid very little attention to providing adequate housing units for its citizens. Thus, in 1972 the Gadhafi government claimed that the regime of King Idris had completed only 6,000 housing units for low-income families in the entire 18 years of rule. However, Gadhafi has promised to confront the problem with vigor and great urgency. But specific information on the improvement of the situation is not available. It is therefore not possible to determine whether he has made good on his promise or not. Nonetheless, if we go by the amount of funds budgeted for housing (over 5 percent of the national budget) we are tempted to say that the housing situation is improving under the Gadhafi administration.

With regard to literacy, we have already noted that the situation of education before and immediately after independence was highly discouraging. In 1951 the literacy rate was about 10 percent (that is, an illiteracy rate of 90 percent). In 1968 the literacy rate had more than doubled to 22 percent. However, since 1971 the Gadhafi government has launched a program designed to eliminate illiteracy within a period of 15 years. We are yet to see the outcome.

CONCLUSION

From the actions and programs of the Gadhafi government, it seems that the goals of his development ideology of Arab-Islamic socialism are gradually being attained. If sheet statistics mean anything, it may be concluded that the average Libyan citizen is benefiting more under the Gadhafi administration than under King Idris. But whether Gadhafi's success in raising the living standards of the Libyans is the result of systematic application of his development ideology, which has been facilitated by the oil wealth, or whether such success would have been possible all the same is a topic that requires thorough investigation and analysis.

NOTES

1. For elaborate details on the theory, see Libyan Arab Republic, The Third International Theory: The Devine Concept of Islam and the Popular Revolution in Libya (Tripoli: Government Printer, 1973).
2. Ibid., p. 15
3. Libyan Arab Republic, First September Revolution and the Contemporary World (Tripoli: Government Printer, 1972), pp. 29-30.

4. Libyan Arab Republic, *The Third International Theory*, op. cit., p. 18.
5. Ibid., p. 18.
6. Libyan Arab Republic, *First September Revolution*, op. cit., p. 30.
7. Ibid., p. 31.
8. Libyan Arab Republic, *The Third International Theory*, op. cit., p. 20.
9. United Nations, *Statistical Yearbook, 1973* (New York: United Nations, 1973), p. 67.
10. Libyan Arab Republic, *Statistical Abstract, 1971* (Tripoli: Government Printer, 1972), p. 27; and R. F. Nyrop, *Area Handbook for Libya* (Washington, D.C.: U.S. Government Printing Office, 1973), pp. 63-64.
11. Nyrop, op. cit., pp. 88, 115.
12. S. A. Hajjaji, *The New Libya: A Geographical, Social, Economic and Political Study* (Tripoli: Government Printer, 1967), p. 82.
13. Ibid., p. 83.
14. Nyrop, op. cit., pp. 115-16.
15. Ibid., p. 116.
16. Hajjaji, op. cit., p. 84.
17. A. N. K. Nair, *Libya's Manpower Resources and Educational and Training Needs 1964-74* (Geneva: International Labor Office, 1974), p. 22.
18. Ibid., p. 20.
19. Ibid., pp. 20-21.
20. Hajjaji, op. cit., pp. 87-88.
21. Nair, op. cit., p. 22.
22. Libyan Arab Republic, *Statistical Abstract, 1973* (Tripoli: Government Printer, 1974), pp. 93-100.
23. World Bank, *Mission Report to Libya, 1959* (Washington, D.C.: World Bank, 1960).
24. Nyrop, op. cit., p. 198.
25. Nair, op. cit., p. 11.
26. International Labor Office, *Survey of North Africa, 1960* (Geneva: ILO, 1961), p. 118.
27. Nyrop, op. cit., p. 62-63.
28. Rawle Farley, *Planning for Development In Libya: The Exceptional Economy in the Developing World* (New York: Praeger, 1971), p. 94.
29. Ibid., pp. 98-99.
30. Nyrop, op. cit., p. 197.
31. Ibid., p. 112; also see Hajjaji, op. cit., p. 107.
32. Libyan Arab Republic, *First African Petroleum Conference, 1974: Nationalization and Participation* (Tripoli: Government Printer, 1974), p. 6.
33. Nyrop, op. cit., pp. 239-51.

34. Ibid. pp. 209-11; also see William C. Wedley "Progress and Problems in the Economic Development of Libya," Libyan Economic and Business Review 4, no. 1 (Spring 1968): pp. 15-18.

35. Wedley, Ibid., pp. 19-20.

36. Nyrop, op. cit., p. 65.

37. ILO Labour Survey of North Africa, 1960, op. cit., pp. 32-33.

38. Nyrop, op. cit., pp. 66-67.

CHAPTER

8

CONCLUSION AND FUTURE PROSPECTS

Certain similarities seem to emerge from this discussion of the various leadership ideologies. Every one of these leaders has declared his intention to develop and to improve the living standards of his people. Whatever ideologies have been formulated by the leaders are therefore geared toward promoting development.

Also each leader has a different reason for adopting a particular ideology. Nyerere, Kaunda, and Khama base their ideologies on traditional African culture and organization. They seek to combine the best from this culture with the modern methods of organization. Gadhafi also returns to Islam to find the basis for his ideology. He aims at combining the humanitarianism implicit in Islam with modern technology to develop his desert country. But Houphouët-Boigny and N'Gouabi depart from this return to tradition. While Houphouët-Boigny goes all out for the free market economy as an ideology for development, N'Gouabi espouses scientific socialism. Each of these two is a doctrinaire believer in his ideology.

Whatever reasons the leaders may have for their development ideologies, their socioeconomic development plans reflect a heavy reliance on socialist principles. All of them emphasize state control of the national economy, an issue that has its pros and cons. The question of whether too much state control and too little scope for private enterprise have, or have not, proved a major obstacle to development efforts has become a topic for debate among development planning experts. Those for little state control argue that in most developing countries the expansion of the public sector has dwarfed that of the private sector during the past decade. The attempts of the developing countries at economic planning almost everywhere have led to intensified central control of economic activity of all kinds. Some think this helps to strangle economic growth. Higher taxation and rising public expenditure mean that too many resources are being diverted from the private sector (where they might have been invested in projects with an economic payoff) and spent on improving administrative and social services as well as public works with no direct economic payoff. Also in many of these countries, in attempting to control the economy directly and to run an unnecessarily large public sector, the state has taken upon itself a task greater than it can handle and a task that exceeds its administrative capacity. Finally, there has been too "heavy" state planning and control and too much reluctance to rely on the mechanisms of the market and the price system. Private initiative as a result has been stifled by lack of incentives and resources and embalmed in red tape. As a result of this, some development planners have advocated liberating the energies of private citizens by opening up the economic participation of private enterprise.

On the other hand, the exponents of state control of the economy argue that to advocate more private enterprise with less state control is to mistake the problem for the solution. Private sectors capable of taking their own investment and management decisions and market price mechanisms to regulate economic growth effectively only emerge at a comparatively advanced stage of development and often after a preparatory period of state control, as in the case of Japan. But in developing countries, where the private sector is weak, internal markets are underdeveloped, and capital is scarce, government must take overall control of investment decisions. The advocates of this point of view strongly object to relying on the play of the market because it cannot be relied upon to bring about the necessary alterations in social and institutional structure. Neither would it be possible to guarantee a more equitable distribution of wealth, which is the object of development.

Whatever arguments are advanced in favor or against, the trend toward government assumption of new functions is likely to continue. This trend is the result of the growth and diffusion of the idea that the state should be responsible for the economic and psychological, as well as well as the physical, security of its citizens. This idea, having gained an ever larger group of adherents, stimulated an active demand that could not be withstood by governments, which by their very nature are conservative. It remains true, however, that if active bodies of opinion demand with sufficient urgency and persistence that a government renders a particular service, or that it imposes a particular control, the realization of these group objectives cannot be long postponed. And in the developing countries such active bodies of opinion are not only numerous but formidable.

Of course, the assumption of social welfare function by the government makes "interference" in private ownership and enterprise inevitable, and the more extensive these functions are, the more thoroughgoing is the "interference." The whole trend has been termed, and properly so, "socialization." This process of socialization continues unabated, for example, in England, under the postwar governments: It has proceeded at a much faster pace than it is now doing in the developing countries of Africa. But the trend in these countries is unmistakable, and it is likely to go on, regardless of which government is in power, military or civilian--and, one might add, regardless of whether the trend is desirable or not.

Thus, although the capitalist state persists outside the Soviet Union and its satellites it does so in a greatly modified form. Many of the features that characterized it in the past either have been irretrievably lost or have changed almost beyond recognition. In one way or another, and usually in a number of ways, the owner of productive properties is held responsible by the state to society at large. How far the process of socialization will run, no development planner and few businessmen would venture to predict. Certain, however, is the fact that differences between allegedly capitalistic nations--such as the United States--and the allegedly socialistic states--such as Soviet Russia--are now only a matter of degree.

The developing countries of Africa may learn from these experiences of the developed nations. Instead of the African leaders preoccupying themselves with doctrinaire socialism and capitalism (as do N'Gouabi and Houphouët-Boigny) they should begin to think of the most practical approaches that would enable them to meet the difficult task of development.

Although most of the leaders stress the socialist approach to development, none of them has yet developed an efficient machinery capable of translating their development ideals into reality. We have indicated that even Tanzania, which seems to have developed such machinery, is finding it difficult to attain her development objectives, let alone socialist Congo, capitalist Ivory Coast, and humanist Zambia, which lack not only the machinery but also skilled manpower to implement their development programs.

Consequently, the numerous programs established to speed the pace of development have not been remarkably successful. Still to be found in each of these countries is a series of social and economic problems such as open unemployment and underemployment, especially in the rural areas where the bulk of the people live and work, as well as uneven distribution of income. Therefore, it is not suprising that all of them stress rural development instead of the colonial strategy of developing pools of modernization such as cities and seaport towns. But despite the emphasis on rural development, there is still a lack of adequate political guidance on the part of the leadership as well as effective state machinery to develop the rural areas. For example, in Zambia, Botswana, and the Congo not much has been achieved in spite of the emphasis given to it in their development plans. Even Tanzania with a comprehensive rural development scheme, the Ujamaa villages, does not seem to have found a proper solution to raising the living standards of her rural poor. We have already alluded to the conflicting reports of the success of the Ujamaa villages.

In spite of their little success with rural development these African economies have shown some appreciable growth since independence.

It is true that more wealth is being produced, but everywhere population increases brought about by modern medicine are checking the hoped-for rise in standards of living. As the distribution of wealth between modern and traditional sectors is notoriously uneven in these countries, it cannot confidently be claimed that "development" has made the average man better off than he was.

The average man has not gained much even with respect to education, which receives considerable emphasis in national development plans. The main educational objective is to wipe out illiteracy and ignorance. But as the statistics on education show, none of the countries seem to be achieving this because of certain factors like the lack of teachers and the paucity or nonexistence of new pedagogical techniques. Nonetheless, these countries' expenditures for education have been rising.

Also the type of education to be developed seems to be of major concern to the African leaders. All of them favor the idea that education should be in step with national needs. We may note that the critical choice between educating for individual enrichment or national development has been a topic of controversy among development planners. The African countries seem to have resolved the dilemma of opting for educating for national development.

As regards health, all the leaders have advocated improvements in health services as well as the eradication of infectious diseases. While progress has been made in nearly all the countries studied, health remains a considerable problem to be tackled. There are still shortages of medical personnel in nearly all of them, which has made countries like the Congo, Zambia, and Tanzania continue to rely on foreign medical experts despite their intention to be self-sufficient. Again, the countries lack the resources and manpower to train sufficient medical personnel of their own. As a result, it is highly probable that they would rely on foreign medical personnel for a long time to come.

Although similiar in some respects, the countries differ in many other aspects, and it is difficult to have a common yardstick to measure the extent of their development. Nearly all the countries have different historical experiences, even though all of them were once colonized. But the style of colonization was different. While countries like the People's Republic of the Congo and the Ivory Coast were under the French colonial rule, others like Zambia, Tanzania, and Botswana were British colonies. Libya has the sad experience of being colonized by Turks, British, French and Italians. These different historical experiences have not only influenced the development paths in these countries but also the ideologies of their respective leaders.

The countries also differ in wealth and infrastructure. While Libya, Zambia, and the Ivory Coast are blessed with some natural resources--such as oil in Libya and copper in Zambia--Botswana and Tanzania are not so lucky. These two countries rely heavily on agriculture. Cocoa-rich Ivory Coast has an additional advantage of inheriting a good infrastructure from the French colonial government. It has not been necessary for her to invest big sums of money in building a good infrastructure, which is a necessary prerequisite for development.

Moreover, some of these countries have experienced various governments and others have had only one government since independence. Libya and the People's Republic of the Congo have changed governments two or three times since independence. Gadhafi came to power after the overthrow of King Idris in a military coup in 1969. And so did N'Gouabi who toppled Massemba-Debat in 1968. Massemba-Debat himself came to power after he successfully ousted the Congo's first president, Abbe Youlou, in a coup d'état in 1963. However, countries like Tanzania, Botswana, Zambia, and the Ivory Coast have each had one government since independence.

From the above discussions of leadership ideology in Africa one question comes readily to mind: What is the possibility that these ideologies would stand the test of time given the fast rate at which governments change in Africa? The change is so frequent that it has become like a game of "musical chairs." As I have observed elsewhere, inherent in this "musical chair" approach to political change is the phenomenon that I call negative competition. By this concept a political leader who succeeds to power tends to do everything possible to obliterate the legacy of his predecessor. The fear that the citizens may tend to compare him to his predecessor, who normally is ousted on charges of corruption or economic mismanagement, is so great that he prefers to outlaw anything that may remind the population of the past.[1]

On the one hand, then, if future African leaders continue to nurture this concept of negative competition, it is very likely that the present leadership ideologies would disappear with their proponents. In effect this means that future leaders may have to start to formulate new development ideologies with probably no tradition to follow except their vague and hazy development notions. But new things are always suspect and they become accepted only with time, if at all. Until the new ideology of a leader is accepted, the country would be operating without any well-defined direction, which the leadership needs to marshal and channel the national efforts of development. And the eventual outcome of all this is underdevelopment.

On the other hand, if the leaders, upon assuming power, decide to conduct a critical evaluation of the legacy of their predecessors in order to decide what to retain and what to discard, then there is a chance that the present ideologies may be continued, possibly with some modifications. Unfortunately, this has not been the case so far. The tendency to be vindictive against deposed leaders still exists. The need and importance attached to a critical examination and evaluation of programs and projects started by ousted leaders are still not the norm in many African countries. Locked in this never-ending morass, one is tempted to conclude that the lifetime of any leadership ideology in Africa will continue to be short. But must Africans continue to live like a "yoyo"?

NOTE

1. See Ukandi G. Damachi, et al., Development Paths in Africa and China (London: Macmillan, 1976), pp. 78-79, for details on this concept.

BIBLIOGRAPHY

Africa Annual Review, 1972. London: Africa Journal Ltd.

Bechuanaland. Report on Localisation and Training. Gaborone: Government Printer, 1966.

Bienefeld, Manfred. "The Informal Sector and Peripheral Capitalism: The Case of Tanzania." Human Resources Research. (Institute of Development Studies Bulletin) 6, no. 3 (February 1975).

Bienen, Henry. Tanzania: Party Transformation and Economic Development. Princeton, N.J.: Princeton University Press, 1970.

Bostock, M. and Harvey, C., eds. Economic Independence and Zambian Copper. New York: Praeger, 1972.

Botswana. National Development Plan 1968-73. Gaborone: Government Printer, 1968.

__________. Statistical Abstract, 1972. Gaborone: Government Printer, 1972.

__________. Statistical Abstract, 1974. Gaborone: Government Printer, 1974.

__________. Ministry of Finance and Development Planning. Manpower and Employment in Botswana. Gaborone: Government Printer, 1973.

__________. National Development Plan, 1973-78, Part I. Gaborone: Government Printer, 1973.

Burke, Fred. "The Search for Ujamaa." In African Socialism. edited by William Friedland and Carl Rosenberg, Jr. Stanford, Calif.: Stanford University Press, 1964.

Culbertson, R. E. Senior Seminar in Foreign Policy: Bechuanaland—Resources for Nationhood and Development. Mimeographed. Washington, D. C.: Foreign Service Institute, 1966.

Damachi, Ukandi G. Nigerian Modernization: The Colonial Legacy. New York: The Third Press, 1972.

__________ et al., eds. Development Paths in Africa and China. London: Macmillan, 1976.

Europa, Africa South of the Sahara, 1974. London: Europa Publications, 1974.

Farley, Rawle. Planning for Development in Libya: The Exceptional Economy in the Developing World. New York: Praeger, 1971.

France. Member States of the French Community. Paris: Government Printer, 1961.

Fraternité February 5, 1960.

Hajjaji, S. A. The New Libya: A Geographical, Social, Economic and Political Study. Tripoli: Government Printer, 1967.

Harbison, F. H. Human Resources as the Wealth of Nations. New York: Oxford University Press, 1973.

__________, Maruhnic, Joan et al. Quantitative Analyses of Modernization and Development. Princeton, N.J.: Princeton University Press, 1970.

__________ and Myers, C. Education, Manpower, and Economic Growth. New York: McGraw-Hill, 1964.

__________. Manpower and Education. New York: Mc-Graw Hill, 1965.

Harvey, Charles. "The Structure of Zambian Development." In Development Paths in Africa and China. Ukandi G. Damachi et al. London, Macmillan, 1976.

Holmes, A. Baron. The International Migration of High-Level Manpower. New York: Praeger, 1970.

Hunter, Guy. Education for a Developing Region: A Study in East Africa. London: Allen and Unwin, 1963.

International Bank for Reconstruction and Development. The Economy of the People's Republic of the Congo: Recent Evolution and Prospects. Mimeographed. November 1971.

International Labor Office. Employment in Africa: Some Critical Issues. Geneva: ILO, 1971.

__________. Survey of North Africa, 1960. Geneva: ILO, 1961.

International Monetary Fund. Surveys of African Economies, Vols. 1, 2 and 3. Washington, D.C.: IMF, 1970.

Iwuji, Eleazar. "Report on Wage/Salary Structures in English-Speaking Africa." In ILO/DANIDA Regional Seminar on Wages. Geneva: International Labor Office, November 1974.

Junod, Violane, ed. Handbook of Africa. New York: Columbia University Press, 1963.

Kaunda, K. Humanism in Zambia. Lusaka: Government Printer, 1967.

__________. Towards Complete Independence: After Mulungushi. Lusaka: Government Printer, 1969.

__________. Zambia's Economic Revolution: The Mulungushi Declaration. Lusaka: Government Printer, 1968.

Kenya. African Socialism and its Application to Planning in Kenya. Nairobi: Government Printer, 1965.

Le Vine, V. T. Political Leadership in Africa. Stanford, Calif.: Stanford University Press, 1967.

Libyan Arab Republic. First African Petroleum Conference, 1974: Nationalization and Participation. Tripoli: Government Printer, 1974.

__________. First September Revolution and the Contemporary World. Tripoli: Government Printer, 1972.

__________. Statistical Abstract, 1971. Tripoli: Government Printer, 1972.

__________. The Third International Theory: The Divine Concept of Islam and the Popular Revolution in Libya. Tripoli: Government Printer, 1973.

Lofchie, M. F. The State of the Nations: Constraints on Development in Independent Africa. Berkeley: University of California Press, 1971.

Lusignan, Guy de. French-Speaking Africa Since Independence. London: Pall Mall Press, 1969.

Mazour, Anatole G. Soviet Economic Development: Operation Outstrip 1921-1965. Princeton, N.J.: D. Van Nostrand, 1967.

Minogue, M. and Molloy, J., eds. African Aims and Attitudes: Selected Documents. Cambridge: Cambridge University Press, 1974.

Mulat, Teshome. "A Review of Income Distribution Questions in Six Eastern African Countries." In East African Regional Workshop on Social Aspects of Employment Promotion. Mimeographed. Geneva: International Institute for Labour Studies, 1975.

Mungner, E. S. Bechuanaland: Pan-African Outpost or Bantu Homeland? London: Institute for Race Relations, 1965.

Nair, A. N. K. Libya's Manpower Resources and Educational and Training Needs 1964-74. Geneva: International Labor Office, 1974.

Nkrumah, Kwame. I Speak of Freedom. London: Heinemann, 1961.

__________. Towards Colonial Freedom: Africa in the War Against World Imperialism. London: Heinemann, 1962.

Nyerere, J. K. Education for Self-Reliance. Dar es Salaam: Government Printer, 1967.

__________. Freedom and Socialism. Oxford: Oxford University Press, 1968.

__________. Socialism and Rural Development. Dar es Salaam: Government Printer, 1967.

__________. Ujamaa: The Basis of African Socialism. Dar es Salaam: Tanganyika Standard, 1962.

Nyrop, R. F. Area Handbook for Libya. Washington, D.C.: U.S. Government Printing Office, 1973.

Oulouguem, Yambo. Bound to Violence. New York: Harcourt, Brace, Jovanovitch, 1971.

People's Republic of the Congo. Directives of the Central Committee of the Congolese Worker's Party for the Planning of Social and

Economic Development in the Popular Republic of the Congo. Mimeographed. Brazzaville, 1973.

__________. Programme du Parti Congolais du Travail. Brazzaville: Government Printer, 1973.

Republic of Zambia. Manpower Report. Lusaka: Government Printer, 1966.

Roberts, T. D. Area Handbook for Ivory Coast. 2 ed. Washington, D. C.: U. S. Department of the Army, 1973.

Routh, Guy. "Development Paths in Tanzania." In Development Paths in Africa and China, Ukandi G. Damachi et al. London: Macmillan, 1976.

Senghor, Lépold Sédar. On African Socialism. New York: Praeger, 1964.

Smit, P. Resources and Development. Pretoria: African Institute of South Africa, 1970.

Statistical and Economic Information Bulletin for Africa, no. 6 (1974).

Stevens, Richard P. Lesotho, Botswana and Swaziland: The Former High Commission Territories in Southern Africa. London: Pall Mall Press, 1967.

Tanganyika Statistical Abstract 1962. Dar es Salaam: Government Printer, 1963.

TANU Constitution. Dar es Salaam: Mwanachi Publishing Co., 1962. (English translation from TANU National Headquarters, mimeographed.)

Tanzania Statistical Abstract. Dar es Salaam: Government Printer, 1970.

Thomas, R. L. Survey of the High-Level Manpower Requirements and Resources for 5-Year Development Plan 1964-65 to 1968-69. Dar es Salaam: Government Printer, 1970.

United Nations. Economic Bulletin for Africa. New York: UN, January 1964.

__________. Statistical and Economic Information Bulletin for Africa. no. 6, 1971.

__________. Statistical Yearbook (Parts 2 and 3) 1973. New York: UN, 1973.

__________. Survey of Economic Conditions in Africa. New York: UN, 1972.

United Republic of Tanzania. Annual Plan for 1972/73. Dar es Salaam: Government Printer, 1972.

__________. Economic Survey 1971-72. Dar es Salaam: Government Printer, 1973.

__________. Survey of Employment and Earnings 1970. Dar es Salaam: Government Printer, 1972.

Wedley, W. C. "Progress and Problems in the Economic Development of Libya." Libyan Economic and Business Review, 4, no. 1 (Spring 1968).

World Bank. Mission Report to Libya, 1959. Washington, D. C.: World Bank, 1960.

Zambia. Second National Development Plan, 1972-1976. Lusaka: Government Printer, 1971.

Zambia. Ministry of Education. Report on Education. Lusaka: Government Printer, August 1969.

ABOUT THE AUTHOR

UKANDI G. DAMACHI is a Staff Associate at the International Institute of Labour Studies, Geneva. He was Hicks Fellow in Industrial Relations at Princeton University, 1970-73, where he also received his Ph. D., a research associate at the Russell Sage Foundation, 1969-70, and an English-speaking Union Scholar to the European Economic Community, 1967. Dr. Damachi has taught at the New School for Social Research and Lincoln University, Pennsylvania, and has done field work in Ghana.

He is author of several books, some of which are Nigerian Modernization: The Colonial Legacy and The Role of Trade Unions in the Development Process: A Case-Study of Ghana, and he has published numerous articles on industrial relations and development.

RELATED TITLES

Published by
Praeger Special Studies

AFRICAN FARMERS: Labor Use in the Development of Smallholder Agriculture
John H. Cleave

CHINESE AND SOVIET AID TO AFRICA
edited by Warren Weinstein

MILITARY RULE IN AFRICA: Dahomey, Ghana, Sierra Leone, and Mali
Anton Bebler

THE ORGANIZATION OF AFRICAN UNITY AFTER TEN YEARS: Comparative Perspectives
edited by Yassin El-Ayouty

PLANNING FOR DEVELOPMENT IN SUB-SAHARAN AFRICA
Ann Seidman

POLITICS IN THE SUDAN: Parliamentary and Military Rule in an Emerging African Nation
Peter K. Bechtold

THE STATUS OF ALIENS IN EAST AFRICA: Asians and Europeans in Tanzania, Uganda, and Kenya
Daniel D. C. Don Nanjira

URBANIZATION, NATIONAL DEVELOPMENT, AND REGIONAL PLANNING IN AFRICA
edited by Salah El-Shakhs and Robert Obudho

U.S. POLICY TOWARD AFRICA*
edited by Frederick S. Arkhurst

*Also available in paperback as a PSS Student Edition.